Readings in Literary Criticism 6
CRITICS ON CHAUCER

Readings in Literary Criticism

CRITICS ON CHAUCER

Readings in Literary Criticism
Edited by Sheila Sullivan

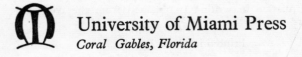

University of Miami Press
Coral Gables, Florida

This edition © George Allen & Unwin Ltd 1970
Library of Congress Catalog Card No. 70-124654
ISBN 0-87024-169-9

Printed in Great Britain

CONTENTS

All quotations throughout the book are from F. N. Robinson's standard edition of Chaucer (listed in the Select Bibliography at the end of this book)

INTRODUCTION

CHAUCER has never fallen from favour in all the five and half centuries since his death. It is a remarkable achievement. There have been times when he was read only by the highly literate, and times when his language and his cheerful bawdiness were condemned as crude or worse. But for those who disapproved of the *fablieu* or the *Prologue* there was always the *Knight's Tale,* or the *Book of the Duchess,* or the *Legend of Good Women.* Today, when we especially prize the sense of actuality, Chaucer in his noblest vein commands less interest than Chaucer the teller of tales, the quizzical onlooker who notices everything but pronounces little. Tomorrow yet other views and aspects will be admired and analyzed. 'Here is God's plenty'— Dryden was writing of the *Canterbury Tales* but his words stand as an epitaph for the whole range of Chaucer's work.

Chaucer's contemporaries admired and copied him. Henry VIII exempted his works (together with the laws of the realm, psalters and prayerbooks) from his 'Act providing for the abolishment of forbidden books'. Ascham approved of him, and Spenser acknowledged him as master and drank deep of his 'well of Englishe undefyled'. Ben Jonson was widely read in Chaucer, and Milton's few comments are all respectful. If there was any time when his poetry fell into some neglect it was in the mid-seventeenth century; but Dryden soon altered that. One of the most vigorous and perceptive of Chaucer's critics, he declared in his Preface to the *Fables* (1700) that he held Chaucer 'in the same degree of veneration as the Grecians held Homer, or the Romans Virgil'. And, believing that Chaucer's language was too antiquated to be generally acceptable, he re-cast several Tales and other passages into the round and polished couplets of his day.

Chaucer was greatly enjoyed in the eighteenth century, but Dryden's view continued to prevail; the language was too rude to be read with pleasure, and the jokes too coarse to be inflicted on ladies. 'I could wish,' wrote John Dart in 1718, 'that Gentlemen would unite their Endeavours to dress him intirely in a more refin'd Habit . . . that he may be fashionable to keep Company with the Ladies.' Of course gentlemen (including Dryden) had done so already, and would do so again. The apparent crudity and obscurity of metre and diction continued for more than another century to be a continual source of worry to Chaucer's admirers. Thomas Urry, in 1721, in perhaps the worst edition of a major poet ever made, evened up the metre, and added and omitted syllables and even words without notice to the reader. And although Pope himself read Chaucer with great pleasure, and regarded him, with Spenser, Milton, and Dryden, as one of the four great landmarks of English poetry, he too re-worked several of the Tales into his own language and metre.

In company with his contemporaries in the Romantic movement (except, surprisingly, for Byron, who recorded some very tetchy words), Wordsworth greatly admired Chaucer. But he too felt the need to modernize, and he in his turn re-fashioned several Tales and other works, including *Troilus*.

Leigh Hunt complained in 1817 of a generally patronizing attitude to Chaucer ('Chaucer is nothing but *old* Chaucer or honest Geoffrey'), and Chesterton in this century made the same complaint. For this Chaucer himself must take a share of the blame. For over five hundred years he has been taken at his own valuation—the amiable narrator, apologetic, frequently bewildered, and himself the most laughable and awkward lover of all. Only in this century has this marvellous creation been fully analyzed, and layer upon layer of irony revealed. Among those who read and study Chaucer an air of patronage is no longer possible. The intriguing problems surrounding the Narrator recur in many of the selections in this book, and there are fuller studies in essays by G. T. Shepherd and Paul Ruggiers.

The point of growth in Chaucer studies came in the mid-nineteenth century, with the founding of the Chaucer Society and the beginning of work on Skeat's six-volume Oxford Chaucer. When the first volumes were published in 1894 they gave an impetus and enthusiasm to Chaucer studies which show no sign of abating. For over fifty years activity on both sides of the Atlantic has been intense. The Americans have taken Chaucer for their own and his debt to American scholarship is vast. I greatly regret having to omit extracts from most of the early American critics, such as G. L. Kittredge, J. M. Manly, R. K. Root, and J. L. Lowes, who have done so much for our understanding of Chaucer. But their works are easily available, and much of their original research and comment has now passed into the groundwork of all Chaucer studies.

I have concentrated chiefly on recent criticism in this book, but I have included extracts from Dryden's essay, which marks the beginning of serious Chaucer criticism, and from Matthew Arnold's praises and strictures, which are answered later in the book by Percy Van Dyke Shelly. Certain other classic studies, such as those by C. S. Lewis, B. L. Jefferson, and W. C. Curry, although not particularly recent, could not be omitted; no more could Virginia Woolf's eagle view of the Chaucer landscape.

The selections include essays on general aspects of Chaucer's poetry, and also one or more critical studies on each of the major works. I have tried to show something of the great diversity of approach, both here and in the USA. For the past few years Chaucer criticism has become less concerned with matters of interpretation and character, and more involved in problems of structure and background. A great deal has been done in the last ten years to clarify the basis of Chaucer's art, and the literary background against which he wrote. R. M. Jordon concerns himself with questions of structure, and essays by D. S. Brewer and J. J. Murphy reveal something of Chaucer's literary background. Although the book partly reflects these recent preoccupations, the essays selected cover a wide range, for they have to follow no less than the range of Chaucer's mind and eye; from the soaring Boethian sweep of *Troilus* to the povre wydwe's sheep that highte Malle.

London, 1970   *Sheila Sullivan*

ACKNOWLEDGEMENTS

We are grateful to the following for permission to use copyright material from the works whose titles follow in brackets:

George Allen and Unwin Ltd and Barnes and Noble (Walter Clyde Curry's *Chaucer and the Medieval Sciences*); Edward Arnold Ltd (A. C. Spearing's *Criticism and Medieval Poetry*); Bertrand H. Bronson and the Modern Language Association of America ('The Book of the Duchess' *Re-opened*); Clarendon Press, Oxford (J. A. W. Bennett's *Chaucer's Book of Fame*; Dorothy Everett's *Essays on Middle English Literature;* C. S. Lewis's *What Chaucer Really Did to* 'Il Filostrato'; and James J. Murphy's *A New Look at Chaucer and the Rhetoricians*); Harvard University Press (R. M. Jordon's *Chaucer and the Shape of Creation*); The Macmillan Co., New York, (Muriel Bowden's *A Commentary on the General Prologue to the Canterbury Tales*); Modern Language Association of America (Charles Muscatine's *Form, Texture and Meaning in Chaucer's 'Knight's Tale*); Thomas Nelson and Sons Ltd and the University of Alabama Press (D. S. Brewer's *Chaucer and the English and European Traditions* and G. T. Shepherd's *The Earlier Poems*); Ruth Nevo and the Modern Language Review '*Motive and Mask in the General Prologue*); New York University Press (W. W. Lawrence's *The Tale of Melibeus* from 'Essays and Studies in Honour of Carleton Brown'); Pennsylvania University Press (Percy Van Dyke Shelly's *The Living Chaucer*); Raymond Preston (*Chaucer*); Princeton University Press (Gordon Hall Gerould's *Chaucerian Essays* and B. L. Jefferson's *Chaucer and the 'Consolation of Philosophy of Boethius'*); University of Wisconsin Press (Paul Ruggiers' *The Art of the Canterbury Tales*); and the late Leonard Woolf and the Hogarth Press Ltd (Virginia Woolf's *The Pastons and Chaucer*).

General Criticism

JOHN DRYDEN

'A perpetual fountain of good sense'

...It remains that I say somewhat of Chaucer in particular. In the first place, as he is the father of English poetry, so I hold him in the same degree of veneration as the Grecians held Homer, or the Romans Virgil. He is a perpetual fountain of good sense.... Chaucer followed Nature everywhere, but was never so bold to go beyond her; and there is a great difference of being *poeta* and *nimis poeta,* if we may believe Catullus, as much as betwixt a modest behaviour and affectation. The verse of Chaucer, I confess, is not harmonious to us; but 'tis like the eloquence of one whom Tacitus commends, it was *auribus istius temporis accommodata:* they who lived with him, and some time after him, thought it musical; and it continues so, even in our judgment, if compared with the numbers of Lidgate and Gower, his contemporaries: there is the rude sweetness of a Scotch tune in it, which is natural and pleasing, though not perfect. 'Tis true, I cannot go so far as he who published the last edition of him; for he would make us believe the fault is in our ears, and that there were really ten syllables in a verse where we find but nine: but this opinion is not worth confuting; 'tis so gross and obvious an error, that common sense (which is a rule in everything but matters of Faith and Revelation) must convince the reader, that equality of numbers, in every verse which we call *heroic,* was either not known, or not always practised, in Chaucer's age. It were an easy matter to produce some thousands of his verses, which are lame for want of half a foot, and sometimes a whole one, and which no pronunciation can make otherwise. We can only say, that he lived in the infancy of our poetry, and that nothing is brought to perfection at the first....

He must have been a man of a most wonderful comprehensive nature, because, as it has been truly observed of him, he has taken into the compass of his *Canterbury Tales* the various manners and humours (as we now call them) of the whole English nation, in his age. Not a single character has escaped him. All his pilgrims are severally distin-

guished from each other; and not only in their inclinations, but in their
very physiognomies and persons. . . .

The matter and manner of their tales, and of their telling, are so
suited to their different educations, humours, and callings, that each
of them would be improper in any other mouth. Even the grave and
serious characters are distinguished by their several sorts of gravity:
their discourses are such as belong to their age, their calling, and their
breeding; such as are becoming of them, and of them only. Some of
his persons are vicious, and some virtuous; some are unlearn'd, or
(as Chaucer calls them) lewd, and some are learn'd. Even the ribaldry
of the low characters is different: the Reeve, the Miller, and the
Cook are several men, and distinguished from each other as much as
the mincing Lady-Prioress and the broad-speaking, gap-toothed Wife
of Bath. But enough of this; there is such a variety of game springing
up before me, that I am distracted in my choice, and know not which
to follow. 'Tis sufficient to say, according to the proverb, that *here
is God's plenty*. We have our forefathers and great-grand-dames all
before us, as they were in Chaucer's days: their general characters
are still remaining in mankind, and even in England, though they are
called by other names than those of Monks, and Friars, and Canons,
and Lady Abbesses, and Nuns, for mankind is ever the same, and
nothing lost out of Nature, though everything is altered. . . .

From 'Preface to the Fables' (1700) in Dryden's *Essays*, (ed. W. P.
Ker), Oxford, 1900, pp. 257–262.

MATTHEW ARNOLD

'Something is wanting'

. . . But in the fourteenth century there comes an Englishman nour-
ished on this poetry, taught his trade by this poetry, getting words,
rhyme, metre from this poetry; for even of that stanza which the
Italians used, and which Chaucer derived immediately from the
Italians, the basis and suggestion was probably given in France.
Chaucer (I have already named him) fascinated his contemporaries,
but so too did Christian of Troyes and Wolfram of Eschenbach.
Chaucer's power of fascination, however, is enduring; his poetical
importance does not need the assistance of the historic estimate; it is
real. He is a genuine source of joy and strength, which is flowing still

for us and will flow always. He will be read, as time goes on, far more generally than he is read now. His language is a cause of difficulty for us; but so also, and I think in quite as great degree, is the language of Burns. In Chaucer's case, as in that of Burns, it is a difficulty to be unhesitatingly accepted and overcome.

If we ask ourselves wherein consists the immense superiority of Chaucer's poetry over the romance-poetry—why it is that in passing from this to Chaucer we suddenly feel ourselves to be in another world, we shall find that his superiority is both in the substance of his poetry and in the style of his poetry. His superiority in substance is given by his large, free, simple, clear yet kindly view of human life,—so unlike the total want, in the romance-poets, of all intelligent command of it. Chaucer has not their helplessness; he has gained the power to survey the world from a central, a truly human point of view. We have only to call to mind the Prologue to *The Canterbury Tales*. The right comment upon it is Dryden's: 'It is sufficient to say, according to the proverb, that *here is God's plenty*.' And again: 'He is a perpetual fountain of good sense.' It is by a large, free, sound representation of things, that poetry, this high criticism of life, has truth of substance; and Chaucer's poetry has truth of substance.

Of his style and manner, if we think first of the romance-poetry and then of Chaucer's divine liquidness of diction, his divine fluidity of movement, it is difficult to speak temperately. They are irresistible, and justify all the rapture with which his successors speak of his 'gold dew-drops of speech'. Johnson misses the point entirely when he finds fault with Dryden for ascribing to Chaucer the first refinement of our numbers, and says that Gower also can show smooth numbers and easy rhymes. The refinement of our numbers means something far more than this. A nation may have versifiers with smooth numbers and easy rhymes, and yet may have no real poetry at all. Chaucer is the father of our splendid English poetry; he is our 'well of English undefiled', because by the lovely charm of his diction, the lovely charm of his movement, he makes an epoch and founds a tradition. In Spenser, Shakespeare, Milton, Keats, we can follow the tradition of the liquid diction, the fluid movment, of Chaucer; at one time it is his liquid diction of which in these poets we feel the virtue, and at another time it is his fluid movement. And the virtue is irresistible.

Bounded as is my space, I must yet find room for an example of Chaucer's virtue, as I have given examples to show the virtue of the great classics. I feel disposed to say that a single line is enough to show the charm of Chaucer's verse; that merely one line like this—

O martyr souded[1] in virginitee!

has a virtue of manner and movement such as we shall not find in all the verse of romance-poetry;—but this is saying nothing. The virtue

[1] The French *soudé;* soldered, fixed fast.

is such as we shall not find, perhaps, in all English poetry, outside the poets whom I have named as the special inheritors of Chaucer's tradition. A single line, however, is too little if we have not the strain of Chaucer's verse well in our memory; let us take a stanza. It is from *The Prioress's Tale,* the story of the Christian child murdered in a Jewry—

> My throte is cut unto my nekke-bone
> Saidè this child, and as by way of kinde
> I should have deyd, yea, longè time agone;
> But Jesu Christ, as ye in bookès finde,
> Will that his glory last and be in minde,
> And for the worship of his mother dere
> Yet may I sing *O Alma* loud and clere.

Wordsworth has modernized this Tale, and to feel how delicate and evanescent is the charm of verse, we have only to read Wordsworth's first three lines of this stanza after Chaucer's—

> My throat is cut unto the bone, I trow,
> Said this young child, and by the law of kind
> I should have died, yea, many hours ago.

The charm is departed. It is often said that the power of liquidness and fluidity in Chaucer's verse was dependent upon a free, a licentious, dealing with language, such as is now impossible; upon a liberty, such as Burns too enjoyed, of making words like *neck, bird,* into a dissyllable by adding to them, and words like *cause, rhyme,* into a dissyllable by sounding the *e* mute. It is true that Chaucer's fluidity is conjoined with this liberty, and is admirably served by it; but we ought not to say that it was dependent upon it. It was dependent upon his talent. Other poets with a like liberty do not attain to the fluidity of Chaucer; Burns himself does not attain to it. Poets, again, who have a talent akin to Chaucer's, such as Shakespeare or Keats, have known how to attain to his fluidity without the like liberty.

And yet Chaucer is not one of the great classics. His poetry transcends and effaces, easily and without effort, all the romance-poetry of Catholic Christendom; it transcends and effaces all the English poetry contemporary with it; it transcends and effaces all the English poetry subsequent to it down to the age of Elizabeth. Of such avail is poetic truth of substance, in its natural and necessary union with poetic truth of style. And yet, I say, Chaucer is not one of the great classics. He has not their accent. What is wanting to him is suggested by the mere mention of the name of the first great classic of Christendom, the immortal poet who died eighty years before Chaucer—Dante. The accent of such verse as

> In la sua volontade è nostra pace ...

is altogether beyond Chaucer's reach; we praise him, but we feel that this accent is out of the question for him. It may be said that it was necessarily out of the reach of any poet in the England of that stage of growth. Possibly; but we are to adopt a real, not a historic, estimate of poetry. However we may account for its absence, something is wanting, then, to the poetry of Chaucer, which poetry must have before it can be placed in the glorious class of the best. And there is no doubt what that something is. It is the σπουδαιότης, the high and excellent seriousness, which Aristotle assigns as one of the grand virtues of poetry. The substance of Chaucer's poetry, his view of things and his criticism of life, has largeness, freedom, shrewdness, benignity; but it has not this high seriousness. Homer's criticism of life has it, Dante's has it, Shakespeare's has it. It is this chiefly which gives to our spirits what they can rest upon....

From 'The Study of Poetry' in *Essays in Criticism* (2nd series, 1880), Everyman edition, 1964, pp. 246–250.

VIRGINIA WOOLF

'What is this world? What asketh men to have?'

... To learn the end of the story—Chaucer can still make us wish to do that. He has pre-eminently that story-teller's gift, which is almost the rarest gift among writers at the present day.... For the story-teller, besides his indescribable zest for facts, must tell his story craftily, without undue stress or excitement, or we shall swallow it whole and jumble the parts together; he must let us stop, give us time to think and look about us; yet always be persuading us to move on. Chaucer was helped to this to some extent by the time of his birth; and in addition he had another advantage over the moderns which will never come the way of English poets again. England was an unspoilt country. His eyes rested on a virgin land, all unbroken grass and wood except for the small towns and an occasional castle in the building. No villa roofs peered through Kentish tree-tops, no factory chimney smoked on the hill-side. The state of the country, considering how poets go to Nature, how they use her for their images and their contrasts even when they do not describe her directly, is a matter of some importance. Her cultivation or her savagery influences the poet far more profoundly

B

than the prose writer. To the modern poet, with Birmingham, Manchester, and London the size they are, the country is the sanctuary of moral excellence in contrast with the town which is the sink of vice. It is a retreat, the haunt of modesty and virtue, where men go to hide and moralize. There is something morbid, as if shrinking from human contact, in the nature worship of Wordsworth, still more in the microscopic devotion which Tennyson lavished upon the petals of roses and the buds of lime trees. But these were great poets. In their hands, the country was no mere jeweller's shop, or museum of curious objects to be described, even more curiously, in words. Poets of smaller gift, since the view is so much spoilt, and the garden or the meadow must replace the barren heath and the precipitous mountainside, are now confined to little landscapes, to birds' nests, to acorns with every wrinkle drawn to the life. The wider landscape is lost.

But to Chaucer the country was too large and too wild to be altogether agreeable. He turned instinctively, as if he had painful experience of their nature, from tempests and rocks to the bright May day and the jocund landscape, from the harsh and mysterious to the gay and definite. Without possessing a tithe of the virtuosity in word-painting which is the modern inheritance, he could give, in a few words, or even, when we come to look, without a single word of direct description, the sense of the open air.

And se the fresshe floures how they sprynge

—that is enough.

Nature, uncompromising, untamed, was no looking-glass for happy faces, or confessor of unhappy souls. She was herself; sometimes, therefore, disagreeable enough and plain, but always in Chaucer's pages with the hardness and the freshness of an actual presence. Soon, however, we notice something of greater importance than the gay and picturesque appearance of the mediaeval world—the solidity which plumps it out, the conviction which animates the characters. . . . Once believe in Chaucer's young men and women and we have no need of preaching or protest. We know what he finds good, what evil; the less said the better. Let him get on with his story, paint knights and squires, good women and bad, cooks, shipmen, priests, and we will supply the landscape, give his society its belief, its standing towards life and death, and make of the journey to Canterbury a spiritual pilgrimage.

This simple faithfulness to his own conceptions was easier then than now in one respect at least, for Chaucer could write frankly where we must either say nothing or say it slyly. He could sound every note in the language instead of finding a great many of the best gone dumb from disuse, and thus, when struck by daring fingers, giving off a loud discordant janlge out of keeping with the rest. Much of Chaucer—a few lines perhaps in each of the Tales—is improper and

gives us as we read it the strange sensation of being naked to the
air after being muffled in old clothing. And, as a certain kind of humour
depends upon being able to speak without self-consciousness of the
parts and functions of the body, so with the advent of decency
literature lost the use of one of its limbs. It lost its power to create
the Wife of Bath, Juliet's nurse, and their recognizable though already
colourless relation, Moll Flanders. Sterne, from fear of coarseness,
is forced into indecency. He must be witty, not humorous; he must
hint instead of speaking outright. Nor can we believe . . . that laughter
of the old kind will ever be heard again.

> But, lord Christ! When that it remembreth me
> Up-on my yowthe, and on my Iolitee,
> It tikleth me aboute myn herte rote.
> Unto this day it doth myn herte bote
> That I have had my world as in my tyme.

The sound of that old woman's voice is still.

But there is another and more important reason for the surprising
brightness, the still effective merriment of the *Canterbury Tales*.
Chaucer was a poet; but he never flinched from the life that was being
lived at the moment before his eyes. A farmyard, with its straw, its
dung, its cocks, and its hens, is not (we have come to think) a poetic
subject; poets seem either to rule out the farmyard entirely or to
require that it shall be a farmyard in Thessaly and its pigs of mythological origin. But Chaucer says outright:

> Three large sowes hadde she, and namo,
> Three kyn, and eek a sheep that highte Malle;

or again:

> A yard she hadde, enclosed al aboute
> With stikkes, and a drye ditch with-oute.

He is unabashed and unafraid. He will always get close up to his
object—an old man's chin—

> With thikke bristles of his berde unsofte,
> Lyk to the skin of houndfish, sharp as brere;

or an old man's neck—

> The slakke skin aboute his nekke shaketh
> Whyl that he sang;

and he will tell you what his characters wore, how they looked, what
they ate and drank, as if poetry could handle the common facts of this
very moment of Tuesday, the sixteenth day of April, 1387, without
dirtying her hands. If he withdraws to the time of the Greeks or the
Romans, it is only that his story leads him there. He has no desire

to wrap himself round in antiquity, to take refuge in age, or to shirk
the associations of common grocer's English.

Therefore when we say that we know the end of the journey, it is
hard to quote the particular lines from which we take our knowledge.
Chaucer fixed his eyes upon the road before him, not upon the world
to come. He was little given to abstract contemplation. He deprecated,
with peculiar archness, any competition with the scholars and divines:

> The answere of this I lete to divynis,
> But wel I woot, that in this world grey pyne is.

> What is this world? What asketh men to have?
> Now with his love, now in the colde grave
> Allone, withouten any companye. . . .

> O cruel goddes, that governe
> This world with binding of your worde eterne,
> And wryten in the table of athamaunt
> Your parlement, and your eterne graunt,
> What is mankinde more un-to yow holde
> Than is the sheepe, that rouketh in the folde?

Questions press upon him; he asks them, but he is too true a poet to
answer them; he leaves them unsolved, uncramped by the solution of
the moment, and thus fresh for the generations that come after him.
In his life, too, it would be impossible to write him down a man of this
party or of that, a democrat or an aristocrat. He was a staunch church-
man, but he laughed at priests. He was an able public servant and a
courtier, but his views upon sexual morality were extremely lax. He
sympathized with poverty, but did nothing to improve the lot of the
poor. It is safe to say that not a single law has been framed or one
stone set upon another because of anything that Chaucer said or wrote;
and yet, as we read them, we are absorbing morality at every pore.
For among writers there are two kinds: there are the priests who take
you by the hand and lead you straight up to the mystery; there are
the laymen who imbed their doctrines in flesh and blood and make a
complete model of the world without excluding the bad or laying stress
upon the good.

Chaucer lets us go our ways doing the ordinary things with the
ordinary people. His morality lies in the way men and women behave
to each other. We see them eating, drinking, laughing, and making
love, and come to feel without a word being said what their standards
are and so are steeped through and through with their morality. There
can be no more forcible preaching than this where all actions and
passions are represented, and instead of being solemnly exhorted, we
are left to stray and stare and make out a meaning for ourselves. It is
the morality of ordinary intercourse, the morality of the novel, which
parents and librarians rightly judge to be far more persuasive than
the morality of poetry.

And so, when we shut Chaucer, we feel that without a word being said the criticism is complete; what we are saying, thinking, reading, doing, has been commented upon. Nor are we left merely with the sense, powerful though that is, of having been in good company and got used to the ways of good society. For as we have jogged through the real, the unadorned country-side, with first one good fellow cracking his joke or singing his song and then another, we know that though this world resembles, it is not in fact our daily world. It is the world of poetry. Everything happens here more quickly and more intensely, and with better order than in life or in prose; there is a formal elevated dullness which is part of the incantation of poetry; there are lines speaking half a second in advance what we were about to say, as if we read our thoughts before words cumbered them; and lines which we go back to read again with that heightened quality, that enchantment which keeps them glittering in the mind long afterwards. And the whole is held in its place, and its variety and divagations ordered by the power which is among the most impressive of all— the shaping power, the architect's power. It is the peculiarity of Chaucer, however, that though we feel at once this quickening, this enchantment, we cannot prove it by quotation. From most poets quotation is easy and obvious; some metaphor suddenly flowers; some passage breaks off from the rest. But Chaucer is very equal, very even-paced, very unmetaphorical. If we take six or seven lines in the hope that the quality will be contained in them it has escaped.

> My lord, ye woot that in my fadres place,
> Ye dede me strepe out of my povre wede,
> And richely me cladden, o your grace
> To yow broghte I noght elles, out of drede,
> But feyth and nakedness and maydenhede.

In its place that seemed not only memorable and moving but fit to set beside striking beauties. Cut out and taken separately it appears ordinary and quiet. Chaucer, it seems, has some art by which the most ordinary words and the simplest feelings when laid side by side make each other shine; when separated, lose their lustre. Thus the pleasure he gives us is different from the pleasure that other poets give us, because it is more closely connected with what we have ourselves felt or observed. Eating, drinking, and fine weather, the May, cocks and hens, millers, old peasant women, flowers—there is a special stimulus in seeing all these common things so arranged that they affect us as poetry affects us, and are yet bright, sober, precise as we see them out of doors. There is a pungency in this unfigurative language; a stately and memorable beauty in the undraped sentences which follow each other like women so slightly veiled that you see the lines of their bodies as they go—

And she set down hir water pot anon
Biside the threshold in an oxe's stall.

And then as the procession takes its way, out from behind peeps the
face of Chaucer, in league with all foxes, donkeys, and hens, to mock
the pomps and ceremonies of life—witty, intellectual, French, at the
same time based upon a broad bottom of English humour.

From 'The Pastons and Chaucer' in *The Common Reader* (1st
series), Hogarth Press, 1925, pp. 24–34.

A. C. SPEARING

An Audience of Listeners

...most medieval poetry was not written, like most modern poetry,
to be read silently by a private individual from the printed page; it was
written to be read aloud to a communal audience of listeners. This
fact is of course well known,[1] and so are its causes. The most important
causes are, first, that in the Middle Ages most writers' audiences would
contain a high proportion of illiterate people, and, second, that before
the invention of printing manuscripts were too expensive for most
people to be able to afford them, whether they could read or not. It
must be added that throughout the medieval period literacy was gradually spreading. In England by the fourteenth century there existed a
literate lay public large enough to call for the various vernacular
devotional works of that period—those of Rolle, Hilton, and the author
of *The Cloud of Unknowing*. Nevertheless, until the very end of the
Middle Ages books were usually written to be read aloud to a group;
and it takes some effort to recall that precisely this fact puts the
twentieth-century literary critic at a severe disadvantage in dealing
with medieval literature. The 'reading method' of the modern critic
is of course that of the private reader in his armchair, not that of the
listener forming one of a group. The twentieth-century critic is well
equipped for dissecting the concentrated kind of literature that is
normally written for an audience of private readers—readers who are
in a position to pause over single lines and words, to compare one

[1] For more detailed discussion, see H. J. Chaytor, *From Script to Print*,
Cambridge, 1945, and Ruth Crosby, 'Oral Delivery in the Middle Ages',
Speculum XI, 1936, 88–110.

part of a work with another, and to reread passages as often as they like or need in order to grasp complexities of meaning. But a medieval listener was in a quite different position from this. He could not go back over something he failed to understand, and he had to be affected by literature immediately or not at all. It was with such a public in mind that the medieval poets had to write. This is not to say, of course, that all medieval literature is simple and lucid. The Provençal poets practised a style called *trobar clus*, which deliberately aimed at obscurity, while much of Dante's work, to take the supreme example of the greatest medieval poet, is extraordinarily difficult. And it is not to say, either, that medieval listeners to a poem were necessarily in the same helpless position that we should be in nowadays if we had to judge a literary work only from hearing it read aloud. Chaucer, for example, was in the first place a court poet, and his original audience would be made up of cultivated people, much more practised than we are in the art of listening, and presumably more competent at it. But, despite all these reservations, the fact is that most medieval English literature was written to have an immediate effect on an audience of listeners. . . .

One result we have certainly noticed already; it is simply that the typical medieval literary work tends to be rather diffuse. We shall see below how medieval theories about literature encouraged diffuseness, and how Chaucer came to be praised by his readers in the later Middle Ages as a miracle of conciseness. Chaucer is indeed probably the most concise of medieval English poets; and yet, compared with more modern poets, he seems extremely diffuse, especially in early works such as *The Book of the Duchess*. He had to be diffuse if his listening audience were to be able to respond to his words. The attention of his audience moves in a linear fashion, from one verse to the next, with no chance to compare or contrast; and so at any particular point the texture must be thin—the poetic effects must be cumulative, extended in time. This means that the modern critic, to be fair to the poem, must try to consider long passages as wholes, and not always expect to find the effect of the whole present locally.

Another result of the fact that medieval literature was orally delivered is that, as compared with poetry of the age of print, more of the poet's meaning must be conveyed through the *sounds* of his verse. These sounds are often those of speech itself. This is noticeable particularly in alliterative poetry, where the freedom of rhythm permits of a close approximation to the rhythms of speech. Poems such as *Sir Gawain and the Green Knight* or *Piers Plowman* are full of exclamations and interjections—words like 'What!', 'Wy!', 'Lo!' 'Baw!', and so on. The greatest English poets of the fourteenth century, whether alliterative or not, are masters of dramatic speech; however magnificent their rhetoric, they fall naturally into the rhythm and idiom of speech at crucial points in their poems. The descriptive passage from

The Book of the Duchess which we have just been looking at does not illustrate this; but at the heart of *The Book of the Duchess* lies human encounter, expressed in dialogue between the Dreamer and the man in black, and the climax of the poem comes in an utterly lifelike interchange of short phrases, including many exclamations:

> *Man in Black:* God wot, allas! ryght that was she!
> *Dreamer:*   Allas, sir, how? what may that be?
> *Man in Black:* She ys ded!
> *Dreamer:*   Nay!
> *Man in Black:*   Yis, be my trouthe!
> *Dreamer:*   Is that youre los? Be God, hyt ys routhe!
> (1307–10)

When Chaucer wants to express violent physical action, he normally does so directly through violence of sound. It has often been pointed out how he makes use of alliteration for this purpose; for instance, he describes the fatal tournament in *The Knight's Tale* as follows:

> Ther *sh*yveren *sh*aftes upon *sh*eeldes thikke;
> He feeleth thurgh the herte-spoon the prikke.
> Up *sp*ryngen *sp*eres twenty foot on highte;
> Out goon the *s*werdes as the *s*ilver brighte;
> The *h*elmes they to*h*ewen and toshrede;
> Out *br*est the *bl*ood with *st*ierne *st*remes rede;
> With *m*yghty *m*aces the bones they to*br*este.
> He *th*urgh the *th*ikkeste of the *th*rong gan *th*reste;
> Ther *st*omblen *st*eedes *st*ronge, and doun gooth al;
> He rolleth under foot as dooth a bal;
> He *f*oyneth on his *f*eet with his tronchoun,
> And *h*e *h*ym *h*urtleth with *h*is *h*ors adoun.
> (*Canterbury Tales,* I 2605–16)

Here the imagery is of the simplest and most conventional—the swords are as bright as silver, an unhorsed knight rolls underfoot like a ball—and there is little dislocation of natural word-order, and no muscular straining of the sense across the gap between one line and the next, such as we might expect to find in a more recent poem. The genius of the passage lies in the selection of incident, the cinematic rapidity of movement between mass effects and individual sufferings (expressed grammatically in the variation between plural and singular forms), and above all in Chaucer's use of the methods of alliterative poetry. . . .

> Of *br*as they *br*oghten *b*emes, and of *b*ox,
> Of horn, of *b*oon, in whiche they *bl*ewe and powped,
> And therwithal they skriked and they houped.
> (*Canterbury Tales,* VII 3398–400)

Another sign of the importance of sound in medieval literature is the predominance among verbal effects of the simple repetition of words and phrases. More will be said about this below, with reference to *Piers Plowman*, but it may be briefly illustrated here by a quotation from the conclusion of Chaucer's *Troilus and Criseyde:*

> Swich fyn hath, lo, this Troilus for love!
> Swich fyn hath al his grete worthynesse!
> Swich fyn hath his estat real above,
> Swich fyn his lust, swich fyn hath his noblesse!
> Swich fyn hath false worldes brotelnesse! . . .
>
> (V 1828-32)

It would be difficult to imagine a simpler rhetoric than this; though one must note the art with which the homiletic power of the first three 'Swich fyn hath's is unexpectedly intensified by the interrupting variation of the fourth line and the resumption of the original pattern in the fifth. It is clear at least, I think, that this is an oral rhetoric, and demands reading aloud if it is to be fully appreciated. Unfortunately, critics of medieval literature are unlikely to be in a position to have their subject matter read aloud to them.

We now come to a third result of the habit of oral delivery, and one which is closely connected with the thinness of texture of medieval verse. If an audience of listeners is to be able to respond to a poem on a single reading of it, not only must its expressive devices be largely simple, they must also contain a high proportion of the familiar. In such circumstances a poet cannot afford to be too novel, too original, too individual in style: he must keep largely within a stylistic convention which his audience will understand and accept without consideration. Within the staple conventional idiom there will of course still be wide scope for a gifted poet to express his individual vision by gradual shadings, cumulative effects; but not by a persistent use of sharply individual turns of phrase. If he is to keep his audience with him, he must usually describe swords as being as bright as silver, and an unhorsed knight as rolling like a ball. He must aim for much of the time at what Professor I. A. Richards has called 'Stock responses'.[2]. . .

Finally, I must mention one further effect that the habit of oral delivery has on medieval poetry. This is an effect not on texture but on structure. A long poem, composed to be read aloud, must inevitably, since there are limits to the amount that an audience of listeners can accept at one sitting, be composed to be read aloud *in instalments*. This means that a long work, such as, for instance, Chaucer's *Troilus and Criseyde*, will tend to be constructed less as a single whole than as a series of episodes. Each episode will be developed semi-independently, and we shall be unable to find in the complete work the Aristotel-

[2] See I. A. Richards, *The Principles of Literary Criticism*, London, 1924, pp. 202ff.

ian kind of unity which has a single plot as its centre or 'soul'. Even in shorter works, there is a tendency for the progression to be so linear that a story changes shape and meaning halfway through, the beginning being forgotten by the time the end is reached. This seems to happen in some of the *Canterbury Tales*. In *The Wife of Bath's Tale*, for example, we begin with a knight who has been sentenced to death for a brutal rape, but he is pardoned on condition that he finds out what thing it is that women most desire. He is told the answer to this riddle by an ugly old woman, but has to marry her in return. He protests, because she is of low birth as well as old and ugly, but she lectures him on the nature of true nobility, he is eventually reconciled to her, and she suddenly becomes young and beautiful. In the course of the tale, the focus of attention has shifted: the knight's original crime has been forgotten, and the question of nobility and of the ideal marriage-relationship has usurped its place. Similarly, in *The Franklin's Tale*, a story that begins with passionate questioning of God's purposes in the ordering of the world ends as a contest in generosity, between a knight, a squire, and a scholar, with the philosophical questioning neither answered nor dismissed, but simply left behind. The Aristotelian kind of unity, however, with its basis in plot, is not necessarily the only possible kind. . . .

From *Criticism and Medieval Poetry*, Arnold, 1964, pp. 16–25.

PERCY VAN DYKE SHELLY

Against Arnold

. . . Arnold goes on to insist that 'Chaucer is not one of the great classics. He has not their accent. . . . The accent of such verse as

> In la sua volontade è nostra pace

is altogether beyond Chaucer's reach. . . . Something is wanting, then, to the poetry of Chaucer, which poetry must have before it can be placed in the glorious class of the best,' and that something is 'the high and excellent seriousness, which Aristotle assigns as one of the grand virtues of poetry. The substance of Chaucer's poetry, his view of things and his criticism of life, has largeness, freedom, shrewdness, benignity; but it has not this high seriousness. Homer's criticism of life has it, Dante's has it, Shakespeare's has it. It is this chiefly which gives to our spirits what they can rest upon.' . . .

The first thing to be said of all this is that though in general Arnold quoted much in his literary criticism—indeed, it was part of his critical method, and he quoted frequently from Homer, Virgil, Dante, Shakespeare, Milton, and Wordsworth—the quotation here, in the essay on the *Study of Poetry*, of a line and a stanza from the *Prioress's Tale*, is the only quotation from Chaucer to be found in the whole of Arnold's work. We thus have evidence that he had read the *Canterbury Tales*, at least in part, but no evidence that he had read any other work by Chaucer, not even *Troilus and Criseyde* or the *Legend of Good Women*.[1] The impression Arnold gives is that his knowledge of Chaucer is slight and thin. The quotation from the *Prioress's Tale* is far from being the happiest choice he could have made to illustrate Chaucer's verse at its best. Many lines in Chaucer's poetry, even in the *Canterbury Tales*, have more of the grace and melody, the unmistakable accent, of great poetry, than have these. And when Arnold quotes the line from Dante and says that the accent of such verse 'is altogether beyond Chaucer's reach', we wonder just how much he knew about Chaucer's pronunciation, even as late as 1880; and this in spite of what he says in appreciation of Chaucer's 'divine liquidness of diction, his divine fluidity of movement'. There is more than one indication that Arnold was not altogether at ease in reading Chaucer. In his earlier essays *On Translating Homer* (1861–62) he speaks several times of the difficulty of Chaucer's English: 'The diction of Chaucer is antiquated'; 'numbers of Chaucer's words are antiquated for poetry'; 'When Chaucer ... is to pass current among us, to be familiar to us ... he has to be modernized'; 'Chaucer's words ... are yet not thus an established possession of an Englishman's mind.' And in the 1880 essay he writes that Chaucer's 'language is a cause of difficulty for us'. Neither Leigh Hunt nor Landor had such complaints to utter or was embarrassed by the difficulty of Chaucer.

When for example, Hunt comes to the description in the *Knight's Tale* of the great 'Emetreus, the kyng of Inde', with its line

Cam ryding lyk the god of armes, Mars,

he exclaims, 'There's a noble line, with the monosyllable for a climax!' It *is* a noble line, and, if I am not mistaken, in the grand style. Chaucer's poetry contains many a line in the grand style; some

---

[1] The only reference to his reading of Chaucer occurs in a letter dated November 1880, and written while he was at work upon this essay, 'The Study in Poetry'. But it gives no indication as to how much or as to what individual works of Chaucer Arnold had read: 'I have been reading Chaucer a great deal, the early French poets a great deal, and Burns a great deal. Burns is a beast, with splendid gleams, and the medium in which he lived, Scotch peasants, Scotch Presbyterianism, and Scotch drink, is repulsive. Chaucer on the other hand, pleases me more and more, and his medium is infinitely superior.' George W. E. Russell, ed., *Letters of Matthew Arnold*, N.Y., 1895, vol. II, p. 214.

of them, like this, notable for their force and a certain majesty; others more touched with sweetness and tenderness, but in equal degree the perfect expression of the thought and examples of the melody that is so peculiarly Chaucer's own. But in order to appreciate them, to perceive that they *are* in the grand style, one must understand both Chaucer's pronunciation and his prosody. Here are a half dozen of them, set down as separate lines:

> And in a tombe of marbul-stones clere
>
> Of olde Britons, dwellinge in this yle
>
> That Gawain, with his olde curteisye
>
> Doun at the rote of Vesulus the colde
>
> Hir olde povre fader fostred she
>
> O tendre, o dere, o yonge children myne

Such lines come to Chaucer easily and naturally, it seems, for they often occur in passages of rather matter-of-fact narrative. In such a setting their beauty startles and delights us all the more:

> So longe he seyled in the salte se
>
> Of olde stories, longe tyme agoon

They occur even in the fabliaux, the last place where Matthew Arnold would find them:

> The dede sleep, for wery bisinesse
>
> Wery and weet, as beste is in the reyn

Again, when the Pilgrims reach the little town of Bob-up-and-Down and the drunken Cook falls off his horse, Chaucer describes the difficulty they had in getting him up again:

> Ther was a greet showving bothe to and fro,
> To lifte him up, and muchel care and wo,
> So unweldy was this sory palled gost.

Here the last line is worthy of Dante at his best, whether in vivid imagery, in strength of imagination, or in accent and movement. But this example would run foul of Arnold's dogma that 'the subject must be a serious one (for it is only by a kind of licence that we can speak of the grand style in comedy)'.[2]

The high seriousness which Arnold insists upon as necessary to the greatest poetry is no doubt a noble thing, and perhaps it springs, as he says it does, from 'a noble nature'. But to a broader criticism and to a critic possessed of a larger humanity it might well seem to spring from weakness, from too great an intensity and narrowness, from the weakness of taking things too seriously, and of taking one's

[2] Chesterton very happily speaks of Chaucer as 'a humourist in the grand style'.

self too seriously along with everything else. Homer, Dante, Milton, and Wordsworth might have been greater poets even than they are had they possessed a sense of humour. It is uncritical, not to say a little absurd, to degrade or disparage a writer for having a sense of humour. The high seriousness of a Dante, a Milton, a Wordsworth— a persistent, unrelieved, and chronic high seriousness—is impossible to men like Chaucer, Shakespeare, Fielding, Lamb, or Thackeray, not alone because they have a sense of humour, but because of their rich and abundant knowledge of life and the breadth of their sympathies. Where it exists, it is the product, it may be, of a noble nature, but also certainly of an intense egotism and a comparatively pale and bloodless humanity. Milton's soul was like a star and dwelt apart, and it was Wordsworth who so described it.

Arnold concedes that Chaucer's criticism of life has 'largeness, freedom, shrewdness, benignity'. But it has more than this; it has also high seriousness—where high seriousness is called for. The outstanding examples are the *Knight's Tale* and *Troilus and Criseyde.* . . .

In modern times Pater has praised the *Knight's Tale* as a noble and powerful handling of the theme of friendship, and he rightly describes this as 'especially a classical motive'. The poem is conceived and executed in the spirit of the highest art. And of specific passages that illustrate the quality of high seriousness, one may mention the famous death of Arcite, or, at the end of the poem, Theseus's speech on the death of all things. The latter strikes the moral and philosophical note and is obviously and directly a criticism of life. The former is something better than this, a bit of life itself, a very moving and tragic bit of life portrayed with perfect truth and art. Both have 'the high seriousness which comes from absolute sincerity'—the quality Arnold denied to Chaucer and acknowledged only in 'the great classics' he named.

But the supreme example of high seriousness in the poetry of Chaucer is to be found in *Troilus and Criseyde,* in the poem as a whole and in many of its parts. The love of Troilus and Criseyde, set against the background of the siege of Troy, entangled with the enmities and treacheries of war, destined to a tragic end by the gods and a hostile fate, and overshadowed even in its moments of bliss by the impending doom of the city, is one of the triumphant examples of high seriousness in English poetry. And this is true whether we think of high seriousness in its moral or in its artistic aspects. The interest deepens as the story unfolds, the action rises to a higher and higher plane, until in the last book Troilus is revealed as a figure of high tragedy, helpless in the toils of 'fatal destyne', with no hope but to find early death in battle. Moreover, in style and in the handling of details of character and scene Chaucer's art is commensurate with the greatness of his theme.

It is strange that one who laid so much stress as Arnold did upon the importance of the action or the story in great poetry, who wrote that 'the eternal objects of poetry, among all nations, and at all times' are 'actions, human actions' and that 'A great human action of a thousand years ago is more interesting . . . than a smaller human action of today', who praised the Greeks because with them 'the poetical character of the action in itself, and the conduct of it, was the first consideration', who found fault with Keats's *Isabella, or the Pot of Basil* and with the moderns in general because they neglect structure, suffer the action to 'go as it will, with occasional bursts of fine writing and with a shower of isolated thoughts and images'—it is strange that such a critic did not value Chaucer more highly, did not see that Chaucer is the supreme master of the story in English poetry, with as fine an instinct for what will make a great story as art in managing it. When Arnold bids us read the story of Keats's poem in Boccaccio to see 'how pregnant and interesting the same action has become in the hands of a great artist, who above all things delineates his object; who subordinates expression to that which it is designed to express', he is sending us abroad for a model when there was a better one at home, and to a model upon whose art the first great English poet so greatly improved in the very points at issue. Chaucer more than any other English poet 'succeeds in effacing himself and in enabling a whole action to subsist as it did in nature'. And the outstanding instances of his success are the *Knight's Tale* and *Troilus and Criseyde*.

It is strange, too, that Arnold, with his love of the classical, of order and sanity, did not see that order and sanity are of the essence of Chaucer's poetry. 'Sanity,' he exclaims, 'that is the great virtue of ancient literature: the want of that is the great defect of the modern, in spite of all its variety and power.' But it is not wanting in Chaucer. Chaucer is the sanest of English poets. And as Professor Lounsbury said forty years ago, 'Of all the English poets no one is so fully the representative of the Hellenic element as Chaucer. . . . In him . . . can be recognized the Hellenic clearness of vision which saw human nature exactly as it was, and did not lack the courage to depict it.'

Lastly, it is strange that one who defined literature as a criticism of life, who found fault with Shelley's poetry for its 'unsubstantiality', its 'incurable want, in general, of a sound subject-matter' and called him 'that beautiful spirit building his many-coloured haze of words and images

"Pinnacled dim in the intense inane" '

should not have been more responsive to the fullness and truth of life in Chaucer. Again and again in reading Chaucer we realize that it is this quality that constitutes his greatest appeal. In this particular, only Shakespeare has excelled him. His poetry is steeped in life, and his subject-matter is as sound today as Shakespeare's, though two hundred years older—sounder far than Spenser's or Milton's. But

Arnold ignored all this, or sacrificed it to a formula about high seriousness and the grand style. As a result his criticism of Chaucer is open
to the charge of blindness and inconsistency. Probably he never read
Chaucer thoroughly. Perhaps he objected to Chaucer's humour, realism, and occasional coarseness. And yet, one remembers that he gave
high praise to Burns's *Jolly Beggars* and despite its 'hideousness and
squalor' and 'bestiality', pronounced it 'a superb poetic success'. In
any case, Arnold's criticism of Chaucer lacks the weight and authority
its manner seems to give it, and he must be charged with doing less
than justice by one of the greatest of English poets. This is the more
to be regretted because Arnold is on the whole the greatest of modern
English literary critics. . . .

> From *The Living Chaucer,* University of Pennsylvania, and
> Oxford, 1940, pp. 30–37.

J. J. MURPHY

A New Look at Chaucer and the Rhetoricians

THE publication in 1926 of John M. Manly's *Chaucer and the
Rhetoricians* touched off a long series of studies devoted to the thesis
that Chaucer, in composing many of his poetical works, consciously
followed the precepts of what Manly termed 'rhetoricians'. For more
than three decades, this thesis has gone substantially unchallenged.[1]

Studies after Manly tend to support one or more of the three
major propositions: first, that Chaucer's use of certain terms proves
his knowledge of formal (i.e. classical) rhetoric; second, that he knew

[1] More than forty such studies have appeared, in addition to a number of
doctoral dissertations. The following examples may provide an illustration of
their direction: C. S. Baldwin, 'Cicero on Parnassus', *P.M.L.A.*, xlii (1927),
106–12; C. O. Chapman, 'Chaucer on Preachers and Preaching', ibid., xliv
(1929), 178–85; R. B. Daniels, 'Figures of Rhetoric in John Gower's English
Works' (unpublished Ph.D. dissertation, Yale University, 1934); D. Everett,
'Some Reflections on Chaucer's "Art Poetical" ', in *Essays on Middle English
Literature,* Oxford, 1955, pp. 149–74; R. C. Goffin, 'Chaucer and Elocution',
M.Æ., iv (1935), 127–42; M. P. Hamilton, 'Notes on Chaucer and the Rhetori-
cians', *P.M.L.A.*, xlvii (1932), 403–9; B. S. Harrison, 'The Colours of
Rhetoric in Chaucer' (unpublished Ph.D. dissertation, Yale University, 1932);
C. Jones, 'The Monk's Tale: a Medieval Sermon', *M.L.N.*, lii (1937), 570–2;
C. Shain, 'Pulpit Rhetoric in Three Canterbury Tales', ibid., lxx (1955),
235–45; F. E. Teager, 'Chaucer's Eagle and the Rhetorical Colours', *P.M.L.A.*,

and used as guides the works of so-called medieval rhetoricians, especially Geoffrey of Vinsauf; and finally, that even if he does not acknow-
ledge them as sources, he relied upon the medieval *artes poetriae*, or
verse-writing manuals, for his knowledge of *colores* or figures. It is the
purpose of this paper to re-examine these propositions under two head-
ings: first, rather briefly, in the light of what is known of the English
rhetorical tradition in the fourteenth century; and, more fully, in the
light of Chaucer's text itself.

It should be noted at once that most investigators have limited themselves to a consideration of these texts contained in Edmond Faral's
Les Arts poétiques du XIIe et du XIIIe siècles (Paris, 1924). Further,
and more significantly, they have assumed that such texts were readily
available in fourteenth-century England. None of the studies, to the
best of my knowledge, has proceeded on the basis of a complete survey
of medieval rhetoric, or from a comprehensive investigation of the
trivium in England during Chaucer's lifetime. It might be fruitful,
therefore, to examine first the status of rhetoric in England at that
period, before assessing the probability of its influence on an individual
writer.

First of all, it would seem that there is very little evidence of an
active rhetorical tradition in fourteenth-century England. Neither
educational records, library catalogues, nor literary allusions provide
any reason for believing that rhetoric in any of its forms played a vital
part in English cultural life during Chaucer's lifetime.

The first concrete evidence of the teaching of formal rhetoric in
English universities, for instance, does not appear until 1431,[2] while
lower schools apparently taught no rhetoric until the fifteenth
century.[3] Library catalogues conspicuously omit medieval rhetorical

[2] An Oxford statute of 1431 is the first known to require the subject for
Inception. Cf. J. J. Murphy, 'The Earliest Teaching of Rhetoric at Oxford',
Speech Monographs, xxvii (1960), 345–7. At Cambridge the date seems to
be even later.

[3] Of the seventy-seven lower schools identified in fourteenth-century England, none records rhetoric as a subject. No complete list of these schools
exists. The fullest list is that of A. F. Leach, *The Schools of Mediaeval England*, New York, 1915, pp. 156–200. Also cf. F. Watson, *The English Grammar School to 1660*, Cambridge, 1908; Leach, *A History of Winchester
College*, London, 1899; L. Thorndike, 'Elementary and Secondary Education
in the Middle Ages', *Speculum*, xv (1940), 400–8; and W. Parry, *Education
in England in the Middle Ages*, London, 1920. Some information on individual
schools is contained in *The Victoria History of the Counties of England*.

xlvii (1932), 410–18. Only one article has urged caution in accepting the
Manly thesis: K. Young, 'Chaucer and Geoffrey of Vinsauf', *M.P.*, xli (1943),
172–82. Since 1943 the tendency has been reinforced by the heavy emphasis
given to Geoffrey of Vinsauf by J. W. H. Atkins, *English Literary Criticism:
The Medieval Phase*, Cambridge, 1943. One by-product of the attention given
to this subject since 1926 is a phenomenon of literary scholarship which it
might be fair to call the 'Cult of Vinsauf'.

texts, and list very few classical treatises.[4] In the derivative forms of ancient rhetoric—i.e. letter-writing manuals and preaching handbooks—the English of Chaucer's day display originality only in the field of preaching,[5] and for the most part rely upon Italian collections of model letters rather than upon the *artes dictandi* themselves.[6]

It is often assumed, on the other hand, that the complete *trivium* of grammar, rhetoric, and dialectic was studied with varying degrees of emphasis throughout medieval Europe. In fourteenth-century England, however, Aristotle's logical works—especially the *Topica* and *De sophisticis elenchis*—seem to have replaced rhetoric at the university level, while lower schools apparently relied upon such basic grammatical works as the *Graecismus* of Evrard of Béthune,[7] the *De grammatica* of Priscian,[8] and the two primers of Donatus, *Ars maior* and *ars minor*.[9] Less formal teaching in the practical arts of correspondence also proceeded without recourse to traditional rhetorical manuals.[10]

Except for the Chaucerian passages and one passage in Book VII of Gower's *Confessio Amantis*,[11] there are no literary allusions at all in English authors of the century which could fairly be taken to indic-

[4] More than 6,000 books are named by title or author in fourteenth-century English library catalogues or donors' lists. Numerous book-lists from this period have been published by M. R. James, although the most convenient analysis of holdings is to be found in E. A. Savage, *Old English Libraries*, London, 1911.

[5] E.g. Robert of Basevorn, *Forma praedicandi*, and Thomas Waleys, *De modo componendi sermones cum documentis*. Both authors were associated with Oxford in the first half of the century. For texts, see T.-M. Charland, *Artes praedicandi*, Paris, 1936. Ranulph Higden, author of the *Polychronicon*, also compiled an *ars praedicandi* which survives in five manuscripts.

[6] The earliest English *artes dictandi* after that of Peter of Blois (1181) seem to be those of John de Briggis (*c.* 1380), Thomas Sampson (after 1350), Richard Kendale (fl. 1431), and John Blakeney (fl. 1447). But English practice seems to have been based on model collections rather than copies of the Italian manuals. See N. Denholm-Young, 'The Cursus in England', *Collected Papers on Medieval Subjects*, Oxford, 1946, pp. 26–55. For a summary of this situation, see J. J. Murphy, 'Rhetoric in Fourteenth-Century Oxford', *M.Æ.*, xxxiv, 1965, pp. 1–20.

[7] *Eberhardi Bethuniensis Graecismus*, ed. I. Wrobel, Vratislavae, 1887.

[8] Ed. H. Keil, *Grammatici latini*, Leipzig, 1853–80, ii–iii. 1–377.

[9] Ibid., iv. 355–402.

[10] Cf. T. F. Tout, 'Literature and Learning in the English Civil Service in the Fourteenth Century', *Speculum*, iv (1929), 365–89; H. G. Richardson, 'Business Training in Medieval Oxford', *American Historical Review*, xlvi (1940), 259–80; M. D. Legge, 'William of Kingsmill—A Fifteenth-Century Teacher of French in Oxford', in *Studies in French Language and Medieval Literature Presented to Mildred K. Pope*, Manchester, 1939, pp. 241–6; and Denholm-Young, op. cit.

[11] Ll. 1507–1640. The passage is clearly a rough paraphrase of a portion of Book III of the *Tresor* of Brunetto Latini. For a discussion of the passage, see J. J. Murphy, 'John Gower's *Confessio Amantis* and the First Discussion of Rhetoric in the English Language', *P.Q.*, xli (1962), 401–11.

C

34 CRITICS ON CHAUCER

ate any English knowledge or interest in the subject of rhetoric. And, despite the efforts of scholars for more than three decades, no evidence other than Chaucer's apparent allusions seems to have been uncovered which would point to the use of the *artes poetriae* in England.

The situation in respect to *grammatica* was quite different. Medieval grammatical treatises fall into four general groups: first, *ars grammatica* proper, such as the rulebooks of Donatus, Priscian, and Alexandre de Villadieu;[12] second, *ars dictandi*, or prose-writing manuals such as that of Hugh of Bologna;[13] third, *ars rithmica*, or treatises dealing with the use of rhythmical language in letters or hymns, typified by the works of Sion of Vercelli;[14] and finally, *ars metrica* or *ars poetriae*, works dealing with metrical composition: the typical authors are Geoffrey of Vinsauf, Matthew of Vendôme, and John of Garland.[15] All four types of grammatical treatises, it might be noted, discuss *exornationes* (*colores* or *figurae*).[16]

From an examination of available sources, it would appear that the most popular books on the arts of discourse in fourteenth-century England belonged primarily to the first category, that of *ars grammatica* proper. Except for religious or theological works, the *Barbarismus* and *Graecismus* were the most popular books in libraries and schools. The Faculty of Grammar at Oxford, moreover, in a statute promulgated between 1306 and 1344, laid down a programme for the teaching of composition which seems to follow the traditional practices associated with the use of Priscian and Donatus....

Indeed, the ubiquity of grammatical texts and the paucity of rhetor-

[12] Villadieu's treatise is edited by Th. Reichling in *Monumenta germaniae paedogogica*, xii (Berlin, 1893). There is no definitive history of medieval grammar, but see R. H. Robins, *Ancient and Medieval Grammatical Theory in Europe*, London, 1951, pp. 69–90; and M. C. Thurot, 'Notices et extraits de divers manuscrits latins pour servir à l'histoire des doctrines grammaticales au moyen âge', *Notices et Extraits*, xxii (1868), pp. 59–148. The definitions of Thomas of Capua give the typical division of *ars grammatica* into its three species: 'tria sunt genera a veteribus diffinita . . . prosaicum, ut Cassiodori, metricum, ut Virgilii, et rithmicum, ut Primatis', *Die Ars Dictandi des Thomas von Capua*, ed. E. Heller, Heidelberg, 1929, p. 13.

[13] See the texts in L. Rockinger, 'Briefsteller und Formelbücher des elften bis vierzehnten Jahrhunderts', *Quellen und Erörterungen zur bayerischen und deutschen Geschichte*, ix, München, 1863. The tripartite division of *ars grammatica* suffered some strain in the case of those works dealing with rhythmical prose composition, but the standard division was nevertheless maintained.

[14] The best collection of texts is that of G. Mari, *I Trattati medievali di ritmica latina* (Memorie del R. Istituto Lombardo di Scienze e Lettere, xx, Milano, 1899).

[15] In addition to the texts published by Faral, see John of Garland's *De arte prosayca et metrica et ritmica*. The portion dealing with *rithmus* is edited by Mari, op. cit., and the other two parts by Mari in *Romanische Forschungen*, xiii (1902), 885–950.

[16] The *Doctrinale*, for instance, treats 80 figures, and the *Graecismus* 104.

ical texts is so marked in fourteenth-century English records that on this ground alone there might be some reason for supposing that Chaucer and his contemporaries may have participated in a 'grammatical' rather than a 'rhetorical' tradition.

This is no idle distinction, since the manuals of grammatical rules —useful, as Quintilian pointed out, for speaking 'correctly'[17]—deal only with the warp and woof of language itself, not with such matters as organization of parts, levels of style, memory, and oral delivery. These latter were, even in the Middle Ages, subjects for the rhetorician or, at most, the author of an *ars poetriae*. The detailed study given to *colores* or *figurae* in ordinary grammar, on the other hand, may have made it unnecessary to turn to rhetorical works even for this kind of doctrine.[18]

The point to be made here is that we can by no means *assume* the existence of a native English rhetorical tradition during Chaucer's lifetime. The evidence indeed points definitely in another direction. On the face of things, therefore, there would seem little probability that any English writer of the period would be influenced greatly by rhetoric in its several medieval forms. . . .

The most damning defect in the argument for Chaucer's self-conscious use of figures, however, is that medieval rhetoricians and grammarians alike set forth the same *exornationes,* or decorative devices. No one since the time of Donatus has been able to make a satisfactory distinction between those figures proper to grammar and those proper to rhetoric.[19] In fact, medieval writers do not even make careful distinctions between *colores rhetorici* and those other *figurae* which do not belong to that classification; in consequence, *colores rhetorici* becomes a set phrase rather than a technical term with a special meaning. The so-called 'rhetoricians'—grammarians like Vinsauf and Vendôme—do no more than parrot the list of figures originally derived from *ad Herennium* but also available in the encyclopedists. These figures were taught in continental classrooms as part of *grammatica.* The 'grammarians' like Villadieu and Béthune list virtually all of *ad Herennium's exornationes* and add a number of others as well. Even the *Barbarismus,* the simple third book of Donatus's *Ars Maior,* lists more *tropi* than does *ad Herennium.* An author's use of a construction identifiable as *traductio,* therefore, indicates only that he may have gone to school, or read one of a number of books, or used the construction without knowing that it had a technical name.

---

[17] *Institutio oratoria,* I. iv. 2.

[18] Imitation of highly coloured models would, of course, have accomplished the same end.

[19] Some distinction is possible in Renaissance texts, because their writers face the problem directly. No medieval writer even attempted to solve the problem. Cf. Thurot, op. cit., pp. 472 ff. And note the complexity of the charts published by Faral, op. cit., pp. 52–54.

So far as Chaucer is concerned, the most enthusiastic proponents of the Vinsauf theory admit that Chaucer uses no more than about fifty of the figures listed in the *Poetria Nova*. Even if we assume that Chaucer used these devices consciously, he would have found, as has been shown, all or most of them in the ordinary grammatical textbooks, particularly the *Graecismus*, a work which describes and exemplifies thirty *schemata*, twenty-one *tropi*, and twenty-five *preceptiva de prosodia* under the heading *de coloribus rhetoricis*. . . .

Nor do the Latin *artes grammaticae* furnish the only possible sources for the knowledge of 'fine' or 'coloured' language. The highly rhetorical French vernacular literature of his own day could have supplied Chaucer with models for the practical skill which he obviously had developed by 1370 (when he composed the *Book of the Duchess*). If he attended grammar school, he probably spoke and read French in connection with his Latin lessons. If he did not attend a grammar school, on the other hand, but secured his education at court, he was even more likely to have read the fashionable Machaut and Froissart.

That Machaut, Froissart, and Deschamps use the term *rhétorique* in connection with poetry has already been noted, and the Provençal writers who composed *Las Leys d'amors* in 1356 provide further evidence of the French interest in rhetoric.[20] Indeed, the interest was so widespread during the fourteenth century that some French writers used the term *seconde rhétorique* to describe versification, whereas *première rhétorique* denoted prose composition.[21] Deschamps's *L'Art de dictier* (1392), in fact, mentioned unnamed 'autres' who customarily made versification a part of *rhétorique*. His own work is significant partly because it breaks with this tradition and places versification under the art of *musica* rather than under *rhetorica*.[22] In view of Chaucer's familiarity with French poetry, including that based on this kind of rhetorical tradition, we can easily see how he could have acquired a full knowledge of 'coloured' language.

Harrison's comparison of the *Book of the Duchess* with its French sources makes such a conclusion even more probable.[23] For instance, while the manuals recommend *digressio*, it is apparent that Chaucer's digression on music (1158–71) has a close parallel in the digression on music in Machaut's *Remède de Fortune*, 3999–4006. Moroever, Harrison identifies six 'colours' in Chaucer's poem which also appear in the French sources: *annominatio*, or play on words; *superlatio*, or hyperbole; *frequentatio*, or various expression of one idea; *correctio*,

---

[20] Cf. W. Patterson, *Three Centuries of French Poetic Theory, 1328–1630*, Ann Arbor, 1935, i. 35–39.

[21] Cf. *Recueil d'Arts de Seconde Rhétorique*, ed. E. Langlois (Documents inédits sur l'Histoire de France, Paris, 1902), pp. i–vi.

[22] E. Deschamps, *Œuvres complètes*, vii. 266–92.

[23] 'Medieval Rhetoric in *The Book of the Duchess*', *P.M.L.A.*, xlix (1934), 428–42.

or negative statement; and two types of *descriptio, effictio* and *notatio*.[24]

Manly's original argument for Chaucer's use of Vinsauf is based in part upon the assertion that his description of Blanche is 'nothing more than a free paraphrase of lines 563–97 of *Nova Poetria*'.[25] It is possible, however, that Chaucer's description in this case might have come directly from the French sources, just as his descriptions of persons in *Troilus and Criseyde* apparently come from his sources.[26] It might be concluded with some justice, then, that Chaucer's French sources could have furnished him very early in his career with models of the conventional devices which are sometimes ascribed to rhetorical sources.[27]

Taken all in all, then, the available evidence does not seem to support the propositions originally advanced by Manly in 1926. Chaucer's use of certain 'rhetorical' terms merely indicates a generalized knowledge of rhetoric rather than a technical acquaintance with it. His allusion to 'Gaufred' can be traced to Trivet. And since there is abundant reason to believe that he may have secured his knowledge of *figurae* from grammatical works or French models, there seems to be no reason to insist upon Geoffrey of Vinsauf or other so-called rhetoricians as sources of the poet's style. It seems evident that his stylistic education had been completed by the time he wrote the *Book of the Duchess* in 1370, and that he did not thereafter need to call upon the French grammarians or rhetoricians for advice.

[24] A striking similarity exists, for instance, between the repetition of 'my . . . my . . . myn' in *Book of the Duchess*, 1037–40, and the repetition of 'ma . . . mes . . . ma' in Machaut's *Le Dit dou lyon*, 215–21. The rhetorical figure involved is *frequentatio*, or repeated introduction of the same word; alliteration is one of its species.

[25] Manly, *Chaucer and the Rhetoricians*, p. 11.

[26] Cf. L. A. Haselmayer, 'The Portraits in *Troilus and Criseyde*', *P.Q.*, xvii (1938), 220–3, and Robinson, p. 834, note on v. 799 ff. Both scholars note that the portraits of Diomedes, Troilus, and Criseyde follow the usual pattern of *effictio*. Robinson cites Benoît, Boccaccio, and Joseph of Exeter as explicit sources, while Haselmayer names Boccaccio as the chief ʌxemplar. In both cases, the French or Italian source supplies the form, not ʌ rhetorical manual.

[27] It might be noted also that there is little evidence to indicate the poet's familiarity with *ars praedicandi*. The *Pardoner's Tale*, for instance, could well be based on personal observation, while the only other Taɪe close to sermon form (*Parson's Tale*) follows the structure of the thematic sermon so loosely that it is difficult to draw a definite conclusion concerning its formal sources. C. O. Chapman ('The Parson's Tale: A Medieval Sermon', *M.L.N.*, xliii (1928), 229–34) argues that the Tale contains the Theme, Prelocution, and Division found in thematic sermon manuals, but Chaucer's apparent reliance upon such sources as Raymond of Pennaforte could just as easily account for the development of ideas through division; cf. Robinson, pp. 765–6. It might be noted also that while the Tale begins with second person address, it soon shifts to the third person, as if the original plan of presenting an ostensibly oral discourse were forgotten in favour of following a source treatise designed for silent personal reading.

The history of Vinsauf in England is as yet unwritten, but his major influence seems to be in the fifteenth and not the fourteenth century. His first champion in England, Thomas Merke, wrote only *c.* 1405,[28] and it was another century after that before his work was even paraphrased in the English language.[29] It does not seem profitable to perpetuate the 'cult of Vinsauf' in relation to Chaucer.

Chaucer's verbal training is probably as broad as the sources of his material are varied. Our investigations of his linguistic skill should be equally broad. Taking a new look at Chaucer and the 'rhetoricians' is but the first step in this direction.

From 'A New Look at Chaucer and the Rhetoricians', *Review of English Studies*, Vol. XV, 1964, pp. 1–5, 16–20.

R. M. JORDON

Inorganic Art

... Although my discussions of Chaucer's poetry emphasize its visible and tangible structure, the central problem of this study is the relationship between the world Chaucer makes in his fiction and the world he knew in his cosmology and his theology. Though I emphasize structure over doctrine, I try to make clear how closely the two are related, since medieval Christianity posits a rationally structured cosmic hierarchy whose parts are meaningfully disposed along the ascending way to God: the structure itself is divine. But I think we must place structure before divinity in studying the art of a secular poet; otherwise we risk confounding the obvious and turning matter into spirit, which only God—not even Chaucer—can do. We are guided here by Chaucer's very clear practice: for example, the Prioress' Tale is religious, the Miller's Tale is not; the ending of *Troilus* is religious, the body of the work is not. Without denying the poet's Christian bearings, I believe that to see Christian doctrine everywhere is to see too well. Perhaps it can be shown that I substitute

[28] Merke's *De moderno dictamine*, extant in ten manuscripts, quotes Vinsauf extensively, usually by name, and refers several times to sections in the *Poetria Nova* which he does not actually quote. For a discussion of Merke, see J. J. Murphy, 'Rhetoric in Fourteenth-Century Oxford', *M.Æ.*, xxxiv, 1965, pp. 1–20.

[29] By Stephen Hawes, *Passetyme of Pleasure* (c. 1509), ed. W. E. Mead (E.E.T.S., o.s., 173, 1928).

one extreme view for another when I maintain that if doctrine is not universally pervasive, certain structural principles are. But I shall attempt to demonstrate what these principles are and how they shape Chaucer's narrative art, whether the instance be explicitly Christian, implicitly Christian, or secular ...

Clearly a strong sense of the limitations of fiction motivated Chaucer's two most explicit and forthright pronouncements on his own art, the 'Retractions' following the *Canterbury Tales* and the 'Epilogue' of *Troilus and Criseyde*. In both of these statements the poet anxiously questions the bases of his art and condemns all that is not openly conducive to piety and spiritual enlightenment. Chaucer's ultimate criteria define Christian instruction, not what later ages have come to call art. Mistrust of fiction permeates Chaucer's art and manifests itself in more subtle and, I think, more important ways, not only through such explicit statements, which, however fervent, are after all only statements, but also through the structure and style of the poems. Chaucer introduces his two major works, *Troilus* and the *Canterbury Tales*, not as fictions but as history and journalism respectively. And in both cases Chaucer's recurrent insistence upon the 'truth' of his fictions—attested to by his unimpeachable 'auctour' in *Troilus* and by his own unimpeachable eyes and ears in the *Tales* —imparts to the poems an artless 'Chaucerian' quality, a quality that determines the essential nature of Chaucer's art. Of course, all fiction 'pretends' in one way or another to be true, but Chaucer's artifices— and medieval practice in general—are easily misunderstood, for they do not spring from the assumptions that underlie modern concepts of artistic truth. Regarding his poems as finite, limited illusions, the medieval poet developed modes of formalism which in the light of modern theory will seem mechanical and artificial but which in truth express assumptions—about both art and life—which are fundamentally and enduringly human.

The irregularities and inconsistencies of a Chaucerian narrative, particularly the recurrent disruptions of illusion but also other overt evidence of the maker's hand—the exposed joints and seams, the unresolved contradictions, the clashes of perspective—are not simply the signs of primitive genius, as Sidney and Dryden were willing to believe; nor are they trivial stylistic blemishes, as modern advocates of psychological realism and dramatic unity have maintained. They are significant determinants of Chaucer's art, based upon an aesthetic which conceives of art not as an organism, a living plant, but as an inorganic material, a 'veil', as Petrarch and Boccaccio understood it, or in more complex works such as *Troilus*, the *Canterbury Tales*, and, preeminently, the *Divine Comedy*, as a structure possessed of architectonic as well as planimetric dimensions. The role of the artist is not to express himself and not to express a new, unique way of viewing reality, but to shape and adorn the materials of his art. The organicist is likely to regard such an approach to art as frivolous, as lacking 'inspiration' or 'commitment' or 'high seriousness'. I hope this book can dispel such reservations and perhaps offer some insight into the possibilities of inorganic art and into the durable bases of such art in a fundamental human responsiveness to quantitative values. The fact that Chaucer still speaks vitally and delightfully to us—while displaying so many qualities antithetical to our organic idea of literature— justifies us to an extent in celebrating him as a 'modern'. But as I shall be concerned to show, even brief study of a Chaucerian narrative can reveal how much such a view leaves out of account. The critical truth must be that despite the immersion of our culture in an aesthetic which regards 'organic unity' as the measure of art, we are by no means numb to 'inorganic' art, though we may be partially blind to it and largely inarticulate in our responses to it. . . .

The *Canterbury Tales* circulated as a gathering of fragments, as an unfulfilled intention. The degree of artistic frustration suffered on this account by Chaucer we can never know, but I think we can assume it to have been very slight. At least such is the inference to be drawn from our knowledge of Chaucer's working methods, as elucidated by source studies. The important point is that Chaucer was a maker of tales, and in the present case he also made a framework. His method of reconciling the framework and the tales was, by and large, to adjust the external details of substantially complete artifacts. Thus a churl's tale would be brought into conjunction with a churl, and which one would go with which would be largely a matter of external choice rather than of inner inevitability. Though in some instances, notably the Wife of Bath's Prologue and the Pardoner's Prologue and Tale, Chaucer moves toward a more fully inner-motivated development of his material, the prevailing impression is one of sharp edges and unsewn seams. Within his framework Chaucer moved his tales around a good deal, shifting tales from one teller to another—from the Man of Law to himself (the *Melibeus*), from the Wife of Bath to the Shipman, and perhaps from the Friar to the Merchant.[1] Such imperfections of adjustment, and many others as well—some simply textual, others integral to Chaucer's artistic technique, as we shall see—reveal the essential character of Chaucer's art. It is an art of superimpositions, adjustments, accommodations. The Six-Text rearrangement of the Tales does not in itself challenge this view or distort the essentially 'arrangeable' quality of the poem. However, the editors' desire to smooth the road to Canterbury eventuated in a journey Chaucer's pilgrims never made. And the 'roadside drama', which is a further extension of the desire to 'unify' the pieces, eventuates in a poem

---

[1] Baugh offers an excellent summary of these and related problems of teller-tale adjustment in his introduction to the *Canterbury Tales* in *Chaucer's Major Poetry*, New York, 1963, pp. 228–235. See also Robinson's explanatory notes to the tales in question.

Chaucer never wrote. Our study of the principles of medieval aesthetic theory and Gothic structure would rather suggest that the basis for a valid unified view of the *Canterbury Tales* is to be found not in the idea of 'fusion' but in that of 'accommodation'. From a Gothic viewpoint the *Tales* can be understood both as a pilgrimage (literal *and* spiritual) and a compound of tales. The mode of relationship between whole and parts can be one which does not at any time rob the parts of integrity and completeness within their own formal outlines. Nor need the part, in its wholeness and complexity, detract from the integrity of the whole. In order thus to have it both ways, Chaucer's art must pay a price, or so it may seem to the modern reader; the price is hard outlines, imperfect resolutions, exposed seams, contradictory viewpoints—in short, conspicuous absence of the primary attributes of post-Jamesian fiction.

I think the most fundamental of these distinctions between Chaucerian and Jamesian canons of literary art concerns attitude towards fictional illusion. There is ample evidence to indicate that Chaucer was thoroughly indifferent toward a quality which modern theory has conditioned us to regard as indispensable to good fiction, namely, consistent, unbroken illusion. . . .

From *Chaucer and the Shape of Creation*, Harvard University Press and Oxford, 1967, pp. 2–9, 117–118.

D. S. BREWER

Chaucer and the English and European Traditions

. . . All poets need a prepared language and an accepted tradition to begin to write in, or they could not begin at all; a poet's stock-in-trade is words, not 'life' or 'feelings' or 'ideas'. A medieval poet was particularly dependent on a formed verbal tradition; he needed it to help himself, and also to fulfil that other essential demand of the rhetoric of poetry, to communicate with the audience. No poet could stand up in his pulpit before the audience, as medieval poets did,[1] if he was

[1] See the famous '*Troilus* frontispiece' of Corpus Christi College, Cambridge, MS No. 61, many times reproduced, most recently in D. S. Brewer, *Chaucer in his Time*, 1963.

not prepared to use a poetic language with which his audience was reasonably familiar, and which it could be expected to understand and even to like. Such concepts of a recognizable, indeed conventional style, appropriate to both subject-matter and audience, consciously chosen with the desire to communicate interest and pleasure, are remote from most modern theories of poetry. They are the concepts of medieval rhetoric. Before condemning them we should realize that some sort of rhetoric is the basis of any poetry.

In order to recognize Chaucer's inherited style we must look at his earliest piece of independent writing, *The Book of the Duchess*, which must have been composed soon after the death in 1369 of Blanche, Duchess of Lancaster and first wife of John of Gaunt, whom it commemorates. Chaucer was between twenty-five and thirty when he wrote it. The poem is heavily indebted for its subject-matter to the French poet Machaut, and, like Machaut's work, it is written in the general tradition of *Le Roman de la Rose*, of which poem there are several actual reminiscences in the text. But our concern here is with the poetic language. The first fifteen lines are closely imitated from *Le Paradys d'Amour* by Chaucer's contemporary, the chronicler and poet Froissart, who also wrote in the tradition of *Le Roman de la Rose*. Chaucer's poem is thus well within the French tradition. Here are Froissart's and Chaucer's openings side by side.

Je sui de moi en grant merveille	I have gret wonder, *be this lyght*
Comment je vifs quant tant je veille	How that I lyve, for *day ne nyght*
Et on ne point en veillant	I may nat slepe *wel nygh noght*;
Trouver de moi plus traveillant,	I have so many an ydel thoght
Car bien sacies que par veillier	*Purely* for defaute of slep
Me viennent suvent travillier	That, *by my trouthe* I take no kep
Pensees et merancolies	Of nothyng, how hyt *cometh or gooth*,
Qui me sont ens au coer liies	Ne me nys nothing *leef nor looth*
Et pas ne les puis deslyer,	Al is ylyche good to me—
Car ne voeil la belle oublyer	*Joye or sorowe*, wherso hyt be—
Pour quele amour en ce travail	For I have felyng in nothyng,
Je sui entres et tant je veil.[2]	But, as yt were, a mased thyng
	Alway *in poynt* to falle a-doun;
	For sorwful ymagynacioun
	Ys always hooly in my mynde.

There is no attempt at close translation. Chaucer has taken the subject-matter from the French, but not the style. Already we have the characteristic Chaucerian tone of voice, self-confidently self-deprecatory, the half-humorous 'I'. What a contrast with Froissart's style! Froissart has written a direct, well-articulated sentence that winds its way gracefully through the octosyllabic rhyme-scheme. If not notably concise, it is not padded; it is sober, well-languaged, flat. In

2 *Œuvres de Froissart,* ed. M. A. Schelar, Brussels 1870, I, p. 1.

contrast, Chaucer's style is lively, conversational, emphatic, dramatic, stuffed with doublets and alternatives, asseverations that are mild oaths, expletives and parentheses. He seems even to avoid French words. Froissart uses *merveil*, and *marvel* had been long enough borrowed from French to make it easily available, but Chaucer prefers the Old English *wonder*, a more powerful word for amazement, with undertones of distress and atrocity. Mersand emphasizes 'the overwhelmingly Anglo-Saxon proportion' of the poem's vocabulary.[3] Wherever Chaucer uses a French word, it is because there is no English equivalent available. The deliberately *chosen* quality of this apparently slack style may be judged by comparison with the Middle English *The Romaunt of the Rose*, a translation of part of *Le Roman de la Rose*. The earlier part of the *The Romaunt* is probably by Chaucer. The opening passage is notably different in tone from that of *The Book of the Duchess*, with few additional phrases, presumably because the aim was a close translation.

Where did Chaucer get such a style? It often seems to be assumed that he carved it out of French, or that he invented it. Of course he invented it in the sense that only his unique individual genius could have put the words together in precisely that way; but he did not invent English. Nor did he invent the collocations that I have italicized in my quotation of the first few lines of *The Book of the Duchess*. Nor did he invent the general tone of the style. This tone resides in the language as it had been spoken and evolved in the country for nearly a thousand years, and in that artistic formalization of the language which is found in what may be called the Middle English rhyming romances. Chaucer's acquaintance with these romances is well known through his sparkling parody of some of their characteristics in *Sir Thopas*, and some scholars have pointed out how his poetry, being, like the romances, to some extent intended for oral delivery, has a number of their stylistic traits.[4] But it cannot be assumed that Chaucer took his parody from his amused discovery in his maturity of naive

---

[3] J. Mersand, *Chaucer's Romance Vocabulary*, New York, 1937, p. 91. Neither Mersand nor I distinguish here between Anglo-Norman (that dialect of French spoken in England) and Continental French, since the immediate point here is the native *English* origin of Chaucer's style, and the main point later will be the influence of Continental French. Chaucer's consciousness of the difference between Anglo-Norman and Continental French is suggested by his satirical reference to the Prioress's ignorance of 'French of Paris' (*The Canterbury Tales*, 1126). That Anglo-French had begun to be old-fashioned even by the beginning of the century is suggested by Miss M. D. Legge in her valuable *Anglo-Norman Literature and its Background*, 1963, p. 6.

[4] See especially Ruth Crosby, 'Oral Delivery in the Middle Ages', *Speculum*, XL (1936) 88–110; and 'Chaucer and the Custom of Oral Delivery', *Speculum*, XIII (1938) 413–32. Cf. also A. C. Baugh, 'Improvization in the Middle English romance', *Proceedings of the American Philosophical Society* CIII (1959), who illustrates very copiously the frequent formulas in the metrical romances.

rubbish.[5] The romances are in fact very mixed, and some of them are poor stuff; perhaps Chaucer did come to despise them: if he did, he was biting the hand that fed him.

In the opening lines of *The Book of the Duchess* (and continually through the poem, too extensively to quote) he shows the romances to be the source of his first poetic nourishment. The collocation *day-night*, for example, is the most frequently repeated phrase in all the romances. The early couplet version of *Sir Guy of Warwick* (to be referred to as *Guy* I), has six instances.[6] That is not a fault of undue repetitiousness in a poem of 7,036 lines, but along with similar repeated collocations it helps to mark its characteristic diction. The charming Breton lay *Sir Degaré* has two instances of *day-night* in its 1,073 lines,[7] while the later *Sir Degrevant* has no less than fourteen in a total of just under two thousand lines.[8] It is needless to multiply examples. Throughout his work Chaucer uses the phrase, in one form or another, over forty-five times.[9] By contrast Gower, who seems to have been little influenced by the romances, uses the phrase only rarely. Chaucer's loose phrase *wel nygh noght* I have not found in the romances, but it is very typical of their style, which abounds in such redundant phrases as *never nought, wel god sped, ryght noght, never none.* Chaucer's phrase *by my trouthe* is again the type of asseveration in which both the romances and the whole of Chaucer's work abound. A hard-swearing romance is *Guy* I—

'God', quod Gij, 'we ben y-nome!'   (we are captured)
l. 1337

Guy's beloved swears *bi mi trewthe* (l. 405), and Guy himself *bi treuthe mine* (l. 4687). The king in *Degaré* also swears *bi my trewthe* (l. 559). The phrase occurs in the alliterative romances of the Northern and Western tradition, but is used in a different way, and there is no sign that Chaucer was much, if at all, influenced by this literature. Gower, a Kentish man, uses the phrase like Chaucer.[10] The romances have many other similar phrases: *bi me leute,* frequent in *Guy* I,[11] *by my feyth in Eglamour,*[12] and so forth. Chaucer's *cometh or gooth*

---

[5] As seems to be assumed in the valuable essays by L. H. Loomis, 'Chaucer and the Auchinleck MS', *Essays and Studies in Honour of Carleton Brown,* New York, 1940.

[6] *Guy of Warwick,* ed. J. Zupitza, EETS, ES 42, 49, 59, (1875–91), ll. 512, 521, 626, 1707, 1716, 4235.

[7] The most convenient collection of romances is that edited by W. E. French and C. B. Hale, *Middle English Metrical Romances,* New York, 1930. See *Sir Degaré,* ed. French and Hale, ll. 3, 712.

[8] *Sir Degrevant,* ed. French and Hale, ll. 28, 44, 49, 60, 111, 412, 495, 534, 708, 740, 784, 1119, 1645, 1790.

[9] Crosby, *Speculum,* XIII, 422.

[10] *Confessio Amantis* IV, l. 2747, in *Works,* ed. G. C. Macaulay, 1901.

[11] E.g. ll. 916, 1512, 1634, etc., ed. cit.

[12] E.g. *Sir Eglamour,* ed. French and Hale ll. 440, 442, 1066, etc.

is a doublet phrase of a type common in the romances. The more usual phrase is *ride or go*, but *comen and goon* occurs in the romances of the second half of the century, though it is also found in other writings. *Leef nor looth* is a pretty example of the long-lasting continuity of English poetic phrases, though it is not confined to the romances. It is first recorded in *Beowulf*, usually thought to have been composed in the eighth century, and by the fourteenth century it was widely diffused in English poetry.[13] *In poynt* is recorded in the fourteenth century only in the rhyming romances, its first recorded use in prose being by Mandeville about 1400....

All his life Chaucer felt the lack of English to be a hindrance to his poetry.[14] Yet even in this early poem (*The Book of the Duchess*) he already begins to repair the lack, and to enrich or 'augment' English within the predominantly Anglo-Saxon diction. In this poem he introduces no less than fourteen French words into literary English, besides the two new Anglo-French compounds, *chambre-roof* and *maister-hunte*.[15] Five of the new words are taken from his sources; *fers, pervers, poune, soleyn*, and *trayteresse*. Of the others, *embosed, forloyn, founes, lymeres, rechased, relayes, soures*, are connected with hunting. *Rayed* and *tapite* are connected with the decoration of a room; like the words to do with hunting, they belong to the courtly life, and were doubtless in normal colloquial use. Fourteen new words in one poem is a considerable addition to the literary language. There are more to add, if we consider new meanings of words already established in the language. The word 'imagination', already noted, appears to be used to mean 'desire', which Godefroy records first in Froissart's *Chronicles*, and is a sense of the word not noticed in the *NED*. *Imagination* was well established in fourteenth-century English, normally used in serious, often religious contexts, but Chaucer is using it in its most modern courtly sense, according to the most advanced usage of his day.

The sources of Chaucer's new words indicate their quality. The five borrowed direct from his sources give a literary tone, and *perverse* and *soleyn* and *trayteresse* convey a degree of abstraction, subtlety and generality of language which is lacking in the romances, though those that were clearly written late in the fourteenth century begin to have something of it. Chess had been played in the romances, and the earliest use of the word *chek* as Chaucer uses it in *The Book of the Duchess* is recorded in the tail-rhyme *Guy*. But *fers* and *poune*, like

---

[13] *Beowulf*, l. 511; *Havelok*, ed. Skeat and Sisam, (1915) l. 2379; 'Song of Lewes', l. 38, and *Bestiary*, l. 86 (both ed. Dickins and Wilson, *Early Middle English Texts* (1951)); 'On the death of Edward III', ed. Sisam, *Fourteenth-Century Verse and Prose*, 1921. Frequent in Gower.

[14] Cf. *The Complaint of Venus*, l. 80, written when he was old.

[15] Mersand, op. cit., counts twenty-one new words, but his details are not always unquestionable.

the words to do with hunting, suggest a new courtly level in the diction. These words, like Chaucer's use of the word *imagination*, are not due to any immediate literary source; they show that Chaucer tends to take his new vocabulary more from the spoken language of the court than from what was to him the latest literature. . . .

Nothing would be more absurd than to attribute the marvellous flourishing of English poetry in the late fourteenth century—Chaucer, Langland, the *Gawain*-poet, and others—to a recrudescence of 'the folk', redolent of the soil. There were certainly patriotic elements, and certainly the language of the farmyard, so to say—truly basic English—was the foundation. But the romances had had this. What made the difference was the increasing use, as we can detect it in Chaucer's verse and elsewhere, of a language of wider vocabulary of ideas, of intellectual discriminations, of items of luxury, of more sophisticated entertainment, of deeper thought. The resulting potential was given actuality in the range of styles that . . . Chaucer was able to control in *The Canterbury Tales*. Chaucer revolutionized 'poetic diction' by 'augmenting' his English with a vast number of new words of Latin, French, and Italian origin. At first many of these were derived from his literary sources. According to Mersand about seventy per cent of the words ultimately derived from French or Latin in his translation of *Le Roman de la Rose*, presumed to be amongst his earliest works, are from the source. But in *The Book of the Duchess* the proportion of such words is just under thirty per cent. In *The House of Fame*, the next of his important poems, though there are fifty-seven new words from French, Italian or Latin, only *two* were traced by Mersand to a literary source. The proportion in *The Parliament* is higher than in *The House of Fame*, but still lower than in *The Book of the Duchess*. In other words, the huge majority of words introduced by Chaucer into the literary language came from current usage. Mersand (p. 74) says it was ninety per cent. In his large vocabulary of just over eight thousand words, about four thousand are words of ultimately Latin source, and well over a thousand of these Chaucer seems to have been the first to use in the literary language.[16] Three-quarters of his innovations have been retained in the language, which in itself speaks well for his inwardness with the genius of English. Of course, the rhyming romances from which Chaucer started also had a good proportion of words of ultimately Latin derivation, having come through French; Chaucer only extends a practice inherent in the language, but the proportion in the romances seems to be much smaller than in Chaucer.

In respect of language, therefore, Chaucer grafts on to his basic English style, found in the romances, a new diction, more elaborate, learned and formal, though also colloquial. This new diction signalizes

[16] Mersand, op. cit., p. 53.

Chaucer's progressive immersion in European literary culture, first in the poetry of the leading poet of his day, Machaut, and in the dominant poetic influence of his day, *Le Roman de la Rose*. Then there was a progressive broadening; Ovid, and to a less extent Virgil, Statius, and Claudian, were all doubtless cherished from schooldays, though Machaut seems to have given the key to their poetic utilization. *Le Roman de la Rose* had pointed to other Latin authors whom Chaucer makes good use of, such as Macrobius and Boethius, late Romans, and the twelfth-century Alan of Lisle, opening the way to science and philosophy. Italian authors Dante and Boccaccio (though not with the *Decameron*) came to swell the flood. Here is indeed the mighty pressure of the European literary mind flooding English poetry. . . .

From *Chaucer and Chaucerians: Critical Studies in Middle English Literature* (ed. D. S. Brewer), Nelson, 1966, pp. 1–5, 24–28.

Specific Criticism

DOROTHY EVERETT

The *Parlement of Foules*

. . . I want especially to speak of the *Parlement of Foules*, for in it Chaucer seems to me to have made a particularly successful and brilliant use of his pattern of the Love Vision. The *Book of the Duchess* perhaps impresses some modern readers as more charming and delicate, but it has more loose ends. The *House of Fame* has things that seem more obviously Chaucerian (the treatment of the Eagle, for instance), but as a whole it is not a success, and was perhaps left unfinished for that reason. The Prologue to the *Legend of Good Women* can hardly be considered by itself. It needs to be related to *Troilus and Criseyde* on the one hand, since it is in a sense a light-hearted comment on that poem, and on the other to the Legends themselves. The *Parlement of Foules* is recognizable, even today, as the most perfect of Chaucer's Love Visions, and it would certainly have seemed so to Chaucer's contemporaries. Its interest lies in the fact that, although it is highly conventional, it is also, as a whole, highly original.

It is not merely in its basic pattern that it conforms to French models. Most of the ways in which Chaucer fills out the pattern had already been exploited. I shall take some of the major ones.

Chaucer's poem is clearly conceived as a Valentine poem. In his Retractions he calls it 'the book of St Valentine's day, of the Parlement of Briddes'. He tells us that the assembly of birds took place on St Valentine's day, and at the end of the poem the birds praise St Valentine in their roundel. One of the French poets who developed the convention of writing poems to celebrate St Valentine's day was Sir Oton de Graunson, whom Chaucer certainly knew, for he names him as 'floure of hem that make in France' at the end of the *Complaint of Venus*. In Graunson's *Songe sainct Valentin*, the poet, like Chaucer in the *Parlement*, dreams that he sees a great assembly of birds of every kind met to choose their mates. It is possible that Chaucer knew this poem,[1] but even if he did not he must have known some of the

[1] See Haldeen Braddy, *Chaucer and the Poet Graunson*, Lousiana, 1947.

many medieval writings in which a council or parliament of the birds is described.[2]

In the later portion of Chaucer's poem, the part that depicts the parliament of birds, and the part that is often remarked on as most original, there are other features that would be familiar to a contemporary audience. One of these is the debate of the birds. To give an early English example of this device, the *Owl and the Nightingale* is a debate between birds. But it is not only the *form* of the debate that would be familiar: its subject would be equally so. When each of the three tercel eagles in turn claims that he has most right to the lady (the formel), he is debating one of the 'questions of love' that were popular as subjects of discussion in love poetry, and possibly also in real life in courtly circles. This particular question is debated in another work of Chaucer's, when, in the *Knight's Tale*, Palamon and Arcite quarrel about Emily.

There are many other familiar features in the earlier parts of the poem. Chaucer in his introduction, like Guillaume de Lorris at the beginning of the *Roman de la Rose*, thinks of the dream of Scipio and of Macrobius, its famous commentator. I quote from the English translation of the *Roman:*

> This may I drawe to warraunt
> An authour that hight Macrobes,
> That halt nat dremes false ne lees,
> But undoth us the avysioun
> That whilom mette kyng Cipioun.   (A, 6–10)

In the vision itself Chaucer introduces the most common of the mythological or allegorical figures which were customary in love visions: Cupid, Venus, and Nature; and in his description of the Garden of Love there are the familiar personifications—Beauty, Youth, Flattery, Desire, &c.—and the familiar decorative details, such as the lists of trees.

But it is not only in its main formal elements and its contents that the *Parlement* conforms to established literary convention. It does so also in the manner of its expression. The French poets to whom Chaucer was, perhaps, most directly indebted in his Love Visions, Machaut and Froissart, wrote in a style whose principles had been laid down in the early-thirteenth-century treatises on the Art of Poetry, such as Geoffrey de Vinsauf's *Nova Poetria*, or Matthieu de Vendôme's *Ars Versificatoria*.

Chaucer evidently learnt both from the French poets and also directly from the treatises. This can be seen from his description of Blanche in the *Book of the Duchess*. In method this description follows the recipe for a description given by Geoffrey de Vinsauf; but Machaut

---

[2] Cf. Robinson, *The Complete Works of Geoffrey Chaucer*, Cambridge, Mass., 1933, p. 361, for full references.

D

had followed the same recipe in his *Jugement dou Roy de Behaigne*, and Chaucer combines details from both. He uses other devices of the rhetoricians in the *Parlement*. *Contentio*, for example, is used as a figure of words; that is, an idea is expressed by contrasting words:

> For out of *olde* feldes, as men seyth,
> Cometh al this *newe* corn from yer to yere.   (22–23)

As a figure of thought, *contentio* contrasts ideas, often using contrasted words as well, as in:

> For bothe I hadde thyng which that I nolde,
> And ek I nadde that thyng that I wolde.   (90–91)

The Prologue to the *Parlement* opens with several instances of this device, all used to describe love:

> The lyf so short, the craft so long to lerne,
> Th'assay so hard, so sharp the conquerynge,
> The dreadful joy, alwey that slit so yerne:
> Al this mene I by Love.   (1–4)

This kind of device, and many others, Chaucer's French predecessors and Chaucer himself undoubtedly used deliberately, with a consciousness of their nature and of where they had learnt them and had met them in other writers.

But in the *Parlement* and in Chaucer's other Love Visions (and also, I believe, in *Troilus*, and in some, though not all, of the *Canterbury Tales*) such devices are not casually introduced. On the contrary, the whole manner and arrangement of the expression depends on the teaching of the so-called 'rhetorical manuals', or, as I prefer to call them, the 'Arts of Poetry'. This I have tried to show elsewhere,[3] and I will not repeat what I have said there. But a further illustration of Chaucer's methods from the *Parlement* will show how he 'knits' (to use his own word) or co-ordinates his various thoughts. In the first stanza he introduces the subject of love in the indirect way I have just indicated: 'al this mene I by Love'; and he goes on to dwell on the miraculous power and the cruelty of love, of which, though he himself has not experienced it, he has read in books:

> For al be that I knowe nat Love in dede,
> Ne wot how that he quiteth folk here hyre.
> Yit happeth me ful ofte in bokes reede
> Of his myrakles and his crewel yre.
> There rede I wel he wol be lord and syre;
> I dar nat seyn, his strokes been so sore,
> But 'God save swich a lord!'—I can na moore.   (8–14)

This statement leads, by way of a general remark on his habit of

---

[3] See pp. 149 ff., 'Some Reflections on Chaucer's "Art Poetical"'.

reading, to a reference to a particular old book which he had been reading in order, he says, 'a certeyn thing to lerne':

> Of usage—what for lust and what for lore—
> On bokes rede I ofte, as I yow tolde.
> But wherfore that I speke al this? Nat yoore
> Agon, it happede me for to beholde
> Upon a bok was write with lettres olde,
> And therupon, a certeyn thing to lerne,
> The longe day ful faste I redde and yerne.   (15–21)

The suggestion in the words 'a certeyn thing to lerne' is here left unexplained; but it is, I think, taken up again later....

I need not continue this minute analysis of the style and manner of the *Parlement*, but I want to lay stress on one point: that in the composition of such a poem nothing is likely to be unconsidered. On the contrary, one would expect everything to be planned and carefully co-ordinated. So, however apparently haphazard or even incongruous some things may appear to be, it would be dangerous to assume that Chaucer introduced them without good reason.

It has been the fashion with this poem to dismiss most of the early part as literary convention, prettily and even elegantly treated but merely introductory to the debate of the birds, which has been universally, and perhaps extravagantly, praised for its freshness and originality. This, I am sure, is the wrong way to look at the poem. The debate begins at l. 416, and so far as the lesser birds are concerned—and it is in them that the twentieth century delights, not in the tercels, with their formal speeches—it begins a good deal later, at l. 491. The whole poem is only 699 lines long. Are we to suppose that Chaucer, who, in smaller matters wrote with such conscious art, allowed himself to patter on to no purpose—or to little purpose—for about three-quarters of the poem before he, as we arrogantly suppose, 'found himself', and said what he wanted to say? Or, to put the question another way, are we to ignore what *we* think is conventional, and to find meaning and pleasure only in what *we* think is fresh and original?

This surely is not merely to misunderstand the *Parlement* but, what is worse, to misunderstand the whole aim and trend of medieval poetry. Nor do we get much further by spying into the so-called conventional parts and comparing them carefully with other examples of the same thing. We can, of course, remark that in describing the Garden of Love in the *Parlement* Chaucer has turned from the usual French sources to the Italian, and so produced something clearer in detail and more decorative than similar descriptions in the French poets; or we can note that the personified virtues 'Dame Pees ... with a curtyn in hire hond' (240), 'Dame Pacience ... With face pale, upon an hil of sond' (242–3), and the goddess Venus herself, have a particularity reminiscent of contemporary Indian paintings. Such observations may make us more appreciative of the details of Chaucer's work, but they do not help us to an understanding of the poem as a whole; and, again, I think that they tend to run contrary to the spirit, not merely of Chaucer, but of medieval poetry as a whole. For, to the medieval poet, the art of poetry was not the creation of something new, but the much humbler one of the selection, arrangement, and representation of what was known and familiar. At its best this resulted in new combinations and revealed new relations, but it meant that even the good poem was likely to be familiar in all its parts, and that it would be valued for this and would appeal as much by its likeness to what was known as by its difference from it.

The notes to Skeat's or Robinson's text of the *Parlement* make it abundantly clear that Chaucer selected the material from many different sources. In addition to the French poets he used Boccaccio's *Teseida* for the description of the garden and of Venus; he takes the dream of Scipio from the fourth book of Cicero's *Republic,* as preserved to medieval times by Macrobius its commentator; the description of Nature and some suggestions for the birds come from the Latin work *De Planctu Naturae* by Alanus de Insulis. These are his major debts, but there are many others: to Boethius, to Dante, to Ovid.

Was this selection merely haphazard? I think not. On the contrary, I believe that each has its purpose in the whole and that the poem as a whole is as closely co-ordinated as is the expression....

The poem, as I have already noted, opens with a description of love—a fact which at least suggests that love is its subject. Moreover, the artificial phrases of the description indicate that Chaucer is thinking of Courtly Love; 'the craft so long to lerne...' (1), 'the dredful joye' (3). Further, he makes it clear that it is not his own love with which he is concerned: 'For al be that I knowe nat Love in dede' (9); but, as he says, he had often read of loves 'myrakles and his crewel yre' (11). When, therefore, he tells us that he read all day in an old book 'a certeyn thing to lerne', it is reasonable to suppose that this thing was love.

But the dream of Scipio and his vision of the 'blysful place' to which come only those who work for the common good, seems little to his purpose. He suggests this himself when he says that, when he had to stop reading for lack of light, he went to bed

> Fulfyld of thought and busy hevynesse;
> For bothe I hadde thyng which that I nolde,
> And ek I nadde that thyng that I wolde. (89–91)

—that is, he had a vision of true felicity but had learnt nothing about love. The lesson of the book had been 'That he ne shulde hym in the world delyte' (66), which was not what he then wanted.

To the modern reader it is not immediately clear why Chaucer should have chosen to relate this dream at this point, and at such length. But there are several indications of its real significance. The first comes from *Troilus and Criseyde* where, almost at the end of the poem, there are lines remarkably like some in this passage of the *Parlement*:

> And whan that he was slayn in this manere,
> His lighte goost ful blisfully is went
> Up to the holughnesse of the eighthe spere,
> In convers letyng everich element;
> And ther he saugh, with ful avysement,
> The erratik sterres, herkenyng armonye
> With sownes ful of hevenyssh melodie.

> And down from thennes faste he gan avyse
> This litel spot of erthe, that with the se
> Embraced is, and fully gan despise
> This wrecched world, and held al vanité
> To respect of the pleyn felicité
> That is in hevene above.   (*Troilus*, v. 1807–19)

> Thanne axede he if folk that here been dede
> Han lyf and dwellynge in another place.
> And Affrican seyde, 'Ye, withouten drede',
> And that oure present worldes lyves space
> Nis but a maner deth, what wey we trace,
> And rightful folk shul gon, after they dye,
> To hevene; and shewede hym the Galaxye.

> Thanne shewede he hym the lytel erthe that here is,
> At regard of the hevenes quantité;
> And after shewede he hym the nyne speres,
> And after that the melodye herde he
> That cometh of thilke speres thryes thre,
> That welle is of musik and melodye
> In this world here, and cause of armonye.

> Than bad he hym, syn erthe was so lyte,
> And ful of torment and of harde grace,
> That he ne shulde hym in the world delyte.
>   (*Parlement*, 50–66)

In both poems Chaucer is contrasting, or rather making his speaker contrast, the transitory things of earth with the 'pleyn felicité that is in hevene above'. In *Troilus*, a few stanzas later, there is further an explicit contrast between heavenly and earthly love. In the *Parlement* this contrast is never explicitly made, probably because it is on so much smaller a scale and is so much lighter in tone and intention than *Troilus*; but this does not mean that it was not here too in Chaucer's mind.

That we are on the right track seems more certain when we look again at the lines in which Chaucer commented on his reading:

For bothe I hadde thyng which that I nolde,
And ek I nadde that thyng that I wolde.   (90–91)

These lines echo some words spoken by Philosophy in Boethius's
Consolation of Philosophy.[4] Philosophy is discoursing on the difference between true and false felicity. She has just explained to Boethius
that riches and honour do not bring true happiness. 'When you had
riches,' she asks Boethius, 'were you never anxious or sorry?' Boethius
replies that he does not remember that he was ever free from anxiety.
' "And was nat that" quod sche "for that the lakkide somwhat that
thow woldest nat han lakkid, or elles thou haddest that thow noldest
nat han had?" ' Once again, it is clear that Chaucer is thinking of the
contrast between true and false felicity. With this idea at the back
of his mind he proceeds to relate his dream, and it is with this idea in
mind that we should read it.

There is more than one indication that Chaucer's dream of the
Garden of Love is to be related to Scipio's dream of true felicity,
and one result of the juxtaposition of the two visions is that the reader
is made to view the Garden of Love in a special way—ironically,
and with a kind of detachment. Both irony and sense of detachment
are in fact interconnected, and both, to some extent, pervade the whole
poem. The detachment is partly indicated and sustained by Chaucer's
manner of presenting himself. He is, as often in other poems, the
slightly bewildered spectator, sympathetic and well-intentioned, but
never quite understanding what is going on. He tells us at the beginning of the poem that he worships Love, but he is so astounded by
Love's works that when he thinks of him he does not know whether
he is swimming or sinking. He is so 'astoned', again (142), at the
inscriptions over the gate that he has not sufficient sense either to
run away or to go in, and is then told by Africanus that 'this writyng
nys nothyng ment bi the' (158), but only concerns the initiates, Love's
Servants. And at the end of the whole poem Chaucer makes no comment at all on what he has seen, but simply turns again to his books,
hoping, in terms vague enough to suggest that he is still at sea, that
some day his reading will result in a dream that will enable him to fare
better.

This portrayal of himself is in itself ironical, but irony is also suggested by several other things early in the poem: by the fact that it is the
same Africanus who gave such solemn advice to Scipio, who leads
Chaucer into the Garden of Love; by the *two* inscriptions over its
gate which are, as Chaucer says, 'of ful gret difference', the one describing the joys, the other the pains of love, a contrast bringing some
reminder of the earlier one drawn by Africanus between the bliss
of heaven and the miseries of earth. And for those who know the
Divina Commedia there is deeper irony in the reminiscences of it

---

[4] iii, pr. 3; Robinson, p. 401.

which Chaucer introduces when he describes his entry into the Garden. Scipio acts and speaks in a manner which recalls Virgil's actions and words to Dante at the entry to the Inferno. The wording of Chaucer's inscriptions over the gate echoes Dante's inscription over the gate to the Inferno.

At the end of the *Parlement,* when the lesser birds discuss the dilemma of the artistocratic eagles, the irony is obvious enough, not only in their behaviour, but also in their formal speeches. The common-sense but crude comments by which the lesser birds reveal their attitude to Courtly Love may be said to be treated ironically; Chaucer portrays both parties faithfully, but holds the scales equally between them, giving no sign of sympathizing with either.

But he leads up to this more obvious irony gradually, by way of long descriptions, first of the Garden, and then of the two goddesses, Venus and Nature. The significance of the descriptions of the goddesses becomes apparent when we compare them in detail, bearing in mind their significance in medieval writings.

Chaucer shows us Venus lying in a 'privé corner' of her dark temple, filled with the sound of sighs,

> Whiche sikes were engendred with desyr.   (248)

She lies on a bed of gold, her golden hair bound with a gold thread, naked from the breast upward and covered otherwise with a thin 'coverchef of Valence'. Then he describes Nature, who surpasses in beauty all other creatures as the bright summer sun surpasses the star. She sits on a green hill surrounded by flowers, leaves, and branches. Venus is petitioned by the two lovers, whose fate we are not told, and the painted walls of her temple depict the stories of unhappy and frustrated lovers, 'al here love, and in what plyt they dyde' (294). Nature, who, following Alanus, is described as the deputy (vicaire) of the Almighty Lord, who knits all the elements into harmony, is petitioned by all the birds of the air, and at the end of the debate she grants them their desire. We know from Alanus and the writers of his school that Nature represents the general order of things[5] and that in Alanus, *De Planctu Naturae,* she upholds natural love, so that, even without the contrasted petitioners, we might guess that in the goddesses we have a contrast between artificial Courtly Love and the natural love of creature for creature, a contrast which the end of the poem reinforces when, after the debate is over, the aristocratic birds are left without satisfaction, while the lower birds, who know only Nature's rule, are happily united.

This, then, is how I think the poem as a whole should be interpreted: as delicately ironical fantasy on the theme of love and not merely of Courtly Love presented through a series of contrasts, variously achieved.

[5] Cf. *The Allegory of Love,* pp. 94 ff.

It is not mere accident that Chaucer introduces so many examples of the rhetorical device of *contentio,* of contrasted phrases and statements, in this poem. It is, I believe, an indication of how his mind was working when he wrote it. His opening lines suggest that he is going to write about Courtly Love, but he quickly passes on, in the dream of Scipio, to a description of true felicity, and a suggested contrast between it and the delights of the world—a contrast which gains point through the linking of this dream to Chaucer's own dream of the Garden of Love. At the entrance to the Garden the contrast is made between the happy lover who comes to the 'welle of grace, There grene and lusty May shal evere endure' (129–30) and the frustrated lover who is compared to a fish left high and dry in a fish-trap. The Garden itself is beautiful, and its air is so temperate 'That nevere was ther grevaunce of hot ne cold' (205), but there is no happiness in the temple of Venus, and Venus herself seems without pity, unlike Nature who sympathizes with the difficulties of the courtly birds, and is also solicitous for the common birds. If these descriptions are intended to contrast, as I have suggested, Courtly Love and Natural Love, the same contrast is also presented from a rather different viewpoint in the debate of the birds and their fate.

We should not, I am sure, attempt to draw a moral from all this. Above all we should avoid the temptation of saying that Chaucer ridicules Courtly Love in this poem. He presents the aristocratic birds sympathetically, and the irony comes only from seeing how the vulgar birds (who *are* vulgar) react to them. What we *can* say, however, is that the Chaucer who wrote this poem can have been no unthinking devotee of Courtly Love. His courtly audience no doubt wished to hear about Courtly Love, and, perhaps even about some particular courtship, and he gave them what they wanted in a poem that pleased them. But he also showed those who wished to see that there were many ways of looking at love.

If, after reading this poem, we turn to *Troilus and Criseyde,* which we believe to have been written later, we shall not expect to find in that greater poem a simple or straightforward presentation of love, courtly or otherwise, for at least the *Parlement* makes it clear that Chaucer had already thought much, and even deeply, on the subject.

From *Essays on Middle English Literature,* Clarendon Press, Oxford, 1955, pp. 98–114.

The *Book of the Duchess* Re-opened

... Coming now to the Dreamer, we confront a problem of far greater complexity. To be truly defined, he must be studied not in isolation but in several different contexts and relationships: as a person outside and inside the dream; in association with the grieving knight of his dream; as he relates to the poet who drew him; and as he bears upon the human connections between Chaucer and John of Gaunt. It will be easiest to consider these aspects of the character one by one.

First, then, for the person who speaks to us directly as narrator throughout the poem. We meet him, first, engulfed in brooding melancholy, sleepless with 'sorwful ymagynacioun'. It is, we notice, his present condition that he is describing, not a state of mind from which he has fortunately escaped. He has suffered thus, he tells us, for as long as eight years, and has no prospect of recovery. The strange dream that he experienced recently, and that he intends to describe, was only an interruption. The dream is thus framed by, or suspended in, the Dreamer's own melancholy, into which he must be understood to have lapsed again upon awaking. He is resigned and passive about his condition, lost in a gentle wonder that he still lives, but not actively seeking death. It is only natural that his attention should have been caught by the plight of another star-crossed lover, when he happened upon it in a book he had chosen with which to while away the sleepless hours. The story concerned the grief of a queen, Alcyone, whose husband was lost at sea, and who could recover no word of his fate, nor get respite from her longing. The Dreamer's heart went out to her in pity, for he found his own sorrow imaged in hers.

Chaucer has been censured for not finding a closer parallel to John of Gaunt's bereavement. The tale of Ceyx and Alcyone, as he tells it, stresses the wife's grief, not the love of a husband bereft. The poet knew better than to set out the accounts, *seriatim,* of three lorn males. Alcyone breaks the sequence without disturbing the mood. She and the Dreamer are akin in their protracted love-longing, and she and the knight are at one in their grief. Deprivation unites us all, men and women, knights and queens. Unvarying repetition is not needed to drive home this truth.

When we look closely at the narrator—the 'I' inside the poem—it is surprising how little countenance he gives to the view of him that has come to be generally accepted since Kittredge's essay, of a simple-minded man, incapable of mature observation or intelligent response

to experience. No doubt it is perilous to assert, where so much depends
on the tone of voice, that after five hundred years we can always detect
the nuances originally intended. It is at least clear that the narrator is
by no means devoid of humour, and also that his sense of humour
includes himself. It is not a very childlike person who can take so
objective a view of his own predicament that, even while he poignantly
feels it, he can both refer to it and refuse to dwell on it, with the
civility and lack of overemphasis here displayed. It might be Pandarus
himself who is speaking. Eight years is a long time to suffer for love:

> And yet my boote is never the ner;
> For there is physicien but oon
> That may me hele; but that is don.
> Passe we over untill eft;
> That wil not be mot nede be left.   (38–42)

He will talk of his sleeplessness: that, after all, is what leads him to
his proper subject. But as to what causes that condition, the less said
—short of downright rudeness—the better. A glancing, good-
humoured allusion is sufficient: who would wish to harp on his own
chronic illnesses?

Obviously, too, the narrator can repeat a story with verve; witness
the visit of Juno's messenger to the gods of slumber, 'who slept and
did no other work'. The comic aspects of the episode are by no means
lost upon him:

> 'Awake!' quod he, 'who ys lyth there?'
> And blew his horn ryght in here eere,
> And cried 'Awaketh!' wonder hye.
> This god of slep with hys oon ye
> Cast up, axed, 'Who clepeth ther?'
> 'Hyt am I,' quod this messager.   (181–186)

Here is no lack of lively and humorous awareness. Soon after, he
declares—'in my game'—that, rather than die for lack of sleep, he
would give that same Morpheus, or Dame Juno—or anyone else, 'I
ne roghte who'—a fine reward, if they would only put him to sleep.
He had scarcely expressed the wish, when, inexplicably, he did fall
asleep.

Anyone, of course, who wishes to regard the manner of the narrative just reviewed as unsophisticated or childlike is entitled to that
privilege. My present purpose is served if it be granted merely that
it is unnecessary so to read it. Up to the point where the narrator
falls asleep, it would, I think, be difficult to prove any significant
difference in character between him and the narrator of the other
dream-visions. If there is naïveté in the tone of the narrative, it is
such a naïveté as we find in the *Parlement,* the *Hous of Fame,* the
Prologue to the *Legend of Good Women,* and, indeed, woven into the
very texture of all this poet's work. It is a simplicity and freshness

of statement that continually trick us into discounting the subtlety of perception and genuine human wisdom behind it.

But the problem of the narrator increases in complexity as soon as we enter the dream. The dreamlike quality of the narrative sequence has not passed unnoticed: due praise has been paid to this aspect of the poet's ordonnance. The way in which one episode opens into another without the logical connections or transitions: the Dreamer awakened *into* his dream by a burst of bird-song, to find himself on his bed with the morning sun making kaleidoscopic patterns through the windows of his chamber, richly stained with the Troy legend, and all the walls painted with the scenes of the Romance of the Rose; sounds outside of preparations for a royal hunt; the Dreamer's taking his horse at once and joining the party; the recall from the hunt; the disappearance of his horse ('I was go walked fro my tree'); the appearance and vanishing of the puppy—no hunting-dog, certainly; the flowery path through the woods full of wild creatures; the discovery of the handsome knight sitting against a huge oak and lost in grief— all this has the familiar but unforeseen and strange air of a dream.

We may also note subtle differences between the Dreamer's waking and sleeping states of mind. He does not lose his sense of humour nor his lively awareness: for example, his remarks on the heavenly singing of the birds on his chamber-roof—they didn't just open their mouths and pretend to be singing! Each one of them, without considering the cost to his throat, really exerted himself to show his best and happiest art. The Dreamer takes himself quite comfortably for granted as he is. It does not occur to him to reflect—but *we* notice the fact—that he is no longer carrying any of that load of oppressive sorrow under which he fell asleep. By a wonderful leap of psychological insight, and in strict accord with truth rediscovered in our own century, his private grief has been renounced by the Dreamer, to reappear externalized and projected upon the figure of the grieving knight. The modern analyst, indeed, would instantly recognize the therapeutic function of this dream as an effort of the psyche to resolve an intolerable emotional situation by repudiating it through this disguise. The knight is the Dreamer's surrogate; and in this view it would be significant that the force which keeps the surrogate from his lady is the far more acceptable, because decisive and final, fact of death. The train of analysis would lead us to assume, of course, a kindred connection between the lady of the dream and the fair but cruel 'physician' who refuses to work a cure in the Dreamer's waking life. And here it would be noted that the knight's long and rapturous eulogy of his lost lady would serve, in the Dreamer's unconscious, to discharge the latter's sense of guilt for the disloyalty of wishing the death of that Merciles Beaute. The disguise is rendered complete by the surrogate's having perfectly enjoyed his love before death severed them.

Someone will exclaim, ironically, how fortunate for the foregoing argument that Gaunt's Duchess had actually died, so that what the Dreamer desired could correspond with the facts! The taunt, of course, is irrelevant. What we are praising here is a depth of psychological truth that stands scrutiny on the level of basic human nature, making its silent contribution to the strength and consistency of the artifact. The historical Blanche and John of Gaunt and Chaucer await attention; but for the present we are concerned with elements inside the poem—connecting tissues, implicit but latent relations, that work below the surface to establish a convincing artistic unity.

The implied identification between the Dreamer and the knight is confirmed by parallels of repetitive description. Of himself, the Dreamer declares that he marvels he still lives:

> For nature wolde nat suffyse
> To noon erthly creature
> Nat longe tyme to endure
> Withoute slep and be in sorwe.   (18–21)

Of the knight, he says:

> Hit was gret wonder that nature
> Myght suffre any creature
> To have such sorwe, and not be ded.   (467–469)

The vital spirit of each of them has deserted its seat. For himself,

> Defaute of slep and hevynesse
> Hath sleyn my spirit of quyknesse;   (25–26)

and the knight is in the same case:

> his spirites wexen dede;
> The blood was fled for pure drede
> Doun to hys herte, to make hym warm—
> For wel hyt feled the herte had harm.   (489–492)

The Dreamer before falling asleep and the knight when he meets him show a kindred stupefaction, a grief so unrelieved that they fail to make contact with what is passing around them:

> I take no kep
> Of nothing, how hyt cometh or gooth . . .
> For I have felynge in nothyng,
> But, as yet were, a mased thyng,
> Always in poynt to falle a-doun.   (6–7, 11–13)

And the knight failed to observe the Dreamer who stood in front of him and spoke:

> throgh hys sorwe and hevy thoght,
> Made hym that he herde me noght;
> For he had wel nygh lost hys mynde.   (509–511)

Both men are hopeless, and the lesson of resignation is one which each has yet to learn. The knight's sorrow is momentarily assuaged by reminiscences, but it keeps recurring, floods back as he ceases to speak, and surrounds the episode of the meeting. The Dreamer likewise has surcease through the dream; but, as we have remarked, the beginning of his narrative, which is also in a sense the ending, encloses the poem with his melancholy. Each has a psychological and as it were biographical relation with Alcyone, and through her with each other. The story of Alcyone is thus a valuable unifying element in the poem as a whole; and, as we shall see, it is much more.

Out of the Dreamer's instinctive sympathy with the knight is developed the mechanism, subtle but with a surface simplicity, that carries the poem through to its conclusion. The Dreamer observes at once that the knight is in mourning and, approaching him silently, receives the sufficient explanation through the knight's overheard lament, that Death has stolen his bright lady. This is information to which, as a stranger, he has no right; but he cannot bear to leave a man in such grief without making any attempt to comfort him. He comes before him, therefore, and greets him quietly, and as soon as his presence is acknowledged, apologizes for disturbing him. He receives a gracious reply, and proceeds to invent conversation on indifferent matters, carefully avoiding reference to the other's state of grief until he has sanction from the knight's own mouth. 'The hunt is over,' he says; 'so far as I can judge, the hart has escaped.' 'It matters not a whit to me,' replies the knight; 'my thoughts have been far otherwise engaged.' 'That is evident enough,' replies the Dreamer; 'you appear to be sorely oppressed. If you felt like telling me about your trouble, I would do my best to relieve you, believe me; and just to talk might help.'

The Dreamer's tact leaves nothing to be desired; his etiquette is unimpeachable. In reply, the knight makes a long figurative statement of his woeful condition, full of rhetorical paradox, but rather unpacking his heart with conventional words than telling his grief directly— partly, perhaps, out of courtesy to a stranger, and partly because he shrinks from uttering the bare truth. He comes close to it in the avowal that death has made him naked of all bliss. But he prefers to stalk his pain rather than confront it immediately. Yet he is not deliberately concealing his meaning, and certainly expects to be understood. He rails on Lady Fortune in set terms, and says he has played a game of chess with her and lost. She made a sly move and stole his 'fers', checkmating him in the middle of the board ('nel mezzo del cammin') with an insignificant stray pawn. She has left him destitute of joy and longing for death.

The Dreamer finds his tale so pitiable that he can hardly bear it. He fully apprehends the meaning of the figurative language, which after all only confirms what he has already overheard. To suppose him mystified at this point were to credit him with rather less than the intelligence of a normal dog. Yet some of Chaucer's critics appear to have done just that. They write as if the Dreamer thinks the game was an actual chess-game, that the 'fers' was a literal piece on a literal board. How the Dreamer would understand the knight's opponent in a literal sense they do not explain. Fortune in person would be something to see! Obviously, the naming of the knight's opponent forces a figurative meaning upon the game. If the Dreamer fails to understand this, he understands nothing at all. He *must* take 'fers' in a figurative sense; and the reason he accepts the figurative term instead of abandoning it is that the knight as yet has given no sanction for the familiarity that a substitution would imply. Decorum, not bewilderment, forbids the Dreamer's referring to the lady in more literal terms.

With all the necessary facts in his possession, the Dreamer realizes that he must try to rescue the knight from this abject submission to misfortune. He sees two possible ways of proceeding. One is to rouse a spirit of endurance in the sufferer; the other, to seek to reduce the proportions of his loss. He tries each of these in turn, not forgetting but taking advantage of the fact that he yet has more specific knowledge than the knight's conversation so far has justified his admitting. At the very least, he must keep the knight talking, to save him from black despair....

... As the Dreamer had anticipated, the knight's memorabilia of his love, once stirred, begin to pour out in a flood: her gracious demeanour, her dancing, her laugh, her look, her hair, her eyes, her soft speaking, her fair dealing—on and on, as if he could never stop. He finally does, however, declaring: 'This was she who was all my joy, my world's well-being, my goddess; and I was hers wholly and entirely.'

The impetuous panegyric has been good for him, as the Dreamer can see. But ecstatic praise without the personal history still leaves the burden undischarged; and it will be yet better if the knight can be got to tell the story of his love, and perhaps be brought to realize it as a treasure that is his to keep, in the teeth of Time and Fortune. 'By our Lord,' says the Dreamer, 'I don't wonder you were wholly hers. Your love was certainly well placed: I don't know how you could have done better.' 'Done better?' exclaims the knight, forgetting logic at the sacrilege of an implied comparison: 'nor could any one have done so well.' 'I certainly think you're right.' 'Nay, but you must believe it!' 'Sir, so I do,' replies the Dreamer, with the reservation in agreement that will keep things going at this critical juncture: 'I believe that to you she was the best and any one seeing her with your eyes would have seen her as the loveliest of women.' 'With *my* eyes? Nay, but every one that saw her said and swore that she was. And had they not, it wouldn't have changed my devotion. I *had* to love her. But *had to* is silly: I wished, I was bound to love her, because she was the fairest and best; it was a free but inevitable offering. But I was telling you about the first time I ever saw her. I was young and ignorant then, but I determined to do my whole devoir in her service. It did me so much good just to see her, that sorrow couldn't touch me the whole day after. She so possessed my mind that sorrow could make no impression.'

The Dreamer's reply is charming and adroit. Here is the man who has claimed to be Sorrow himself, the essential personification of that state, describing how the idea of his love could heal him of all sorrow. The Dreamer leads him toward self-realization by suggesting, figuratively, how much he had to rejoice over, since he could still think of her. 'You seem to me,' says the Dreamer, 'like a man who goes to confession with nothing to repent.' 'Repent!' cries the knight indignantly, rising to the bait: 'far from me be the thought of repenting my love. That were worse than the worst treason that ever was. No, I will never forget her as long as I live.' The Dreamer does not press the logical victory, but turns back to ask again for the narrative, still not forgetting that the lady's death is a fact that the knight does not know that he possesses. 'You have told me,' says he, 'about your first sight of your lady. I beseech you to tell me how you first spoke to her, and the rest; and about the nature of the loss you have suffered.' 'Yes,' says the knight, 'it's greater than you imagine.' 'How so, sir? Won't she love you? or have you acted in a way that has caused her to leave you? Tell me everything, I pray you.'

With this urging, the knight at last abandons indirections and moves straight down the autobiographical road until he reaches the point of perfect felicity. 'Al was us oon,' he says,

> withoute were.
> And thus we lyved ful many a yere
> So wel, I kan nat telle how. (1295–97)

Too plainly, this is not the end. 'For ever after,' the story-books would say. But in life it is not so, and the Dreamer must help him to his conclusion. 'Sir,' he asks gently, 'where is she now?' 'Now?' repeats the knight, his grief suddenly overwhelming him. 'Alas that I was born! That is the loss I told you of, remember? It was herself.' 'Alas, sir, how?' 'She is dead.' 'Oh, no!' 'She is, though.' 'So that is it. God, how sad!'

There is nothing in this narrative, nor in the dialogue which punctuates it, that need to be taken as insensibility or forgetfulness or egregious simplicity on the part of the Dreamer. To the contrary, it is hard to imagine the situation being handled with more awareness and delicacy by Geoffrey Chaucer, courtier, man of the world, and poet, *in propria persona,* had it confronted him so in actual life. Never presuming on his private knowledge, the Dreamer leads the knight

from point to point to disclose everything, and at the knight's own pace
and pleasure. . . .

Reprinted by permission of the Modern Language Association of
America from 'The *Book of the Duchess* Re-opened', *Proceedings
of the Modern Language Association*, vol. 67, 1952, pp. 865–877.

J. A. W. BENNETT

Chaucer's *Book of Fame*

... ONE effect of the crisp dialogue that precedes the poet's departure
from the castle is to lend perspective to the scenes enacted within it.
It is now evident that the climax of the action lies elsewhere. And it
is time to remember that his first guide had found him deficient not
only in love-tidings but in knowledge of his 'verray neyghebores' at
his doorstep. For at the gate of the castle he sees 'faste by' its workaday
counterpart, a suburb in the strict sense, standing outside (and just
below) the castle wall as huts of thatch and wattle stood outside the
medieval *castellum* yet were part of it, if the perishable part. It is a
single vast house of woven wattle and in perpetual motion, creaking
as if spun round by the wind. In its simple and impermanent materials
there is a distinct suggestion of the primitive. *Primumque furcis erectis
et virgulis interpositis luto parietes texerunt,* says Vitruvius ('at the
beginning they put up rough spars, interwove them with twigs, and
finished the walls with mud').[1] So Virgil, contrasting the elegant
Capitol of his own day and its distant predecessor in Aeneas's time,
speaks of it as 'now roofed with gold, then thatched with thorn' (*Aen.*
viii. 348).

But such hints or suggestions hardly constitute precedents; and
for several features of this house of twigs precedents or parallels are
hard to find. Taken in order of importance the apparently novel
features are:

(i) Its precise location—in a valley, immediately below the hill of
Fame, where it is 'founded to endure Whil that is list to Aventure'
(1981–2)—i.e. built to last for just so long as Chance allows. Here
the association with Aventure provides a clue. For Alanus's house of
Fortune is similarly placed: part is firmly set on the mountain-top
(see p. 106 above), part clings to the mountain-foot, on the verge
of collapse:

> Rupis in abrupto suspensa minansque ruinam,
> Fortune domus in preceps descendit ...
> *(Anticlaudianus,* viii. 1–2)

The 'ruyne' associated with Rumour (1974) must be given the
material sense suggested by these lines—*Casum tanquam lapsura
minatur,* adds Alanus. All the mean and impermanent features in the

---

[1] Quoted by Erwin Panofsky, *Studies in Iconology,* second edition, Oxford,
1962, p. 44.

E

antiphrasis that has earlier contributed to the palace of Fame, Chaucer has reserved for Rumour.

(ii) The style and material of the building. It is the elaborate construction that first excites the visitor's wonder, reflected as that wonder is in the comparison with Daedalus's labyrinth. The essential point of likeness is the intricacy of each structure: as the *multiplex domus* that Daedalus built for Minos had its blind and deceptive passages, a 'conflicting maze of divers winding paths' (*variarum ambage viarum*: *Met.* viii. 161), so this house is skilfully and deliberately built ('queynteliche ywroughte') to provide innumerable entrances, vents, and windows in the interstices of the wicker-work. For Chaucer, as for Virgil and Ovid, Daedalus was *ingenio fabrae celeberrimus artis* (*Met.* viii. 159); and besides the labyrinth and the wings that 'changed the laws of Nature' (ibid. 189) he built, *ut fama est*—'as report has it'—a temple to Apollo. So at least says Virgil, and describes how he set it up at Cumae near the cave of the *horrenda Sibylla* after his ill-fated flight, and depicted on its portal the whole legend of the minotaur:

> hic labor ille domus et inextricabilis error;
> magnum reginae sed enim miseratus amorem
> Dædalus, ipse dolos tecti ambagasque resolvit;
>
> (*Aen.* vi. 27–29)

Thus for the Middle Ages Daedalus was pre-eminently the cunning builder and inventor. Alanus refers to him as the former when describing the attributes of Prudence: *ut Dedalus erigit arces* (*Anticlaudianus*, ii. 352). As the latter he has already appeared in *Fame*, being the wretch whose craft brought disaster on his son (919)—an allusion which must make us chary of interpreting the present allusion as extolling his creative genius à la James Joyce. *Domus Dedali* (1928) recalls Mirk's 'hous of dadull', and may well have a dyslogistic sense.[2] Moreover the effect of the intricate cage-like basketwork is to suggest again a lack of solidity. Even so does Alanus (as seen already) underline the contrast between the two sides of Fortune's house: the one gleaming with gold and adorned with a lofty roof, the other rubbishy and full of holes:

> resplendet pars una domus; pars altera vili
> materie deiecta jacet. Pars ista superbit
> culmine sublimi, pars illa fatiscit hiatu.
>
> (*Acl.* viii. 10–12)

And Jean de Meun had not only elaborated this comparison but deepened the disparity, specifying mud walls thinner than the palm of his

---

[2] 'My howse ys an hous of oresons. But . . . now hit ys made an hous of dadull and of whisperyng and rownyng': Mirk, *Festial* (ed. Erbe), p. 279.

hand, roof of straw, cracks and holes 'more than five hundred thousand':

> S'est toute couverte de chaume
>   . . . . .
> E pourfendue de crevaces
> En plus de cinc cenz mile places.
> *(Roman de la Rose,* 6108–14)[3]

But Jean was still concerned to depict the reverse, and reverses, of Fortune. Chaucer represents the house as of daedal art because, though he has separated Fame from Rumour, he recognized that no great gulf divides them. So his house of Rumour, though accommodating all sorts and conditions of men, and primitive in its materials, is no decayed and dirty hovel; and one detail that in the *Roman* is merely realistic Chaucer invests with both a practical and a symbolic purpose. The French poet roofs the rude structure with straw like a penthouse. Such a hutment would generally be built of wattle, so that osier or willow ('timber of no strengthe', 1980)[4] came to be a proverbial synonym for fragility, witness the Wife of Bath:

> Whoso that buildeth his hous al of salwes
>   . . . . .
> Is worthy to ben hanged on the galwes.
> *(CT,* D. 655 ff.)

Whatever the commentators say, Chaucer would not need to wander in Wales or Ireland to find such dwellings. They were a part of any rural scene, and remained so till Milton pictured the plebeian rout of *Fama* as buzzing like the flies round the shepherds' huts *texta iunco.* Such sheds might indeed be 'shapen lyk a cage' (1985)—or at least like a beehive. Evidently we must think of a skip or cage suspended from the battlements of the castle and so vast that the eagle, when the time comes (2030), can easily enter through one of the apertures. It is tempting, though fruitless, to speculate whether the image was suggested to Chaucer by the cage in which Alexander's birds bore him up through the aerial regions; we can certainly read it as a preparative for the re-entry of the eagle-conductor into the action of the poem: for the next moment Chaucer catches sight of his bird 'perched hye upon a stoon' (1991). Only a bird in flight could offer to show him the inside of the cage—'So faste hit whirleth, lo, aboute'.

(iii) Though a whirling movement might easily be postulated of

---

[3] See further H. R. Patch, *The Goddess Fortuna,* pp. 127–8 and pl. 7. In Spenser the house of Pride, in which Lucifer sits gorgeously enthroned, is craftily built and covered in gold foil, but rests on a sandy foundation 'and all the hinderparts, that few could spie / Were ruinous and old' (*Faerie Queene,* I. iv. 4–5).

[4] The term 'wicker' is first recorded in *OED* in connection with straw used for thatching: *Cal. Doc. Scot.* 1336.

light basket-work hanging in the wind—'As with the wynd wavys the wickir' is Dunbar's symbol for 'warldis vanite' in his 'Lament for the Makers'—the emphasis on the speed of the rotation suggests something supernatural, and scholars have reasonably compared the revolving castles of medieval romance. In the Welsh *Fled Bricrend*, for example, Cúroí's fortress revolves as fast as a millstone after he departs for the skies; and *Arthur of Little Britain* (Lord Berner's version of a composite French text that obviously embodies traditional motifs) includes an account of a similar phenomenon.[5] Yet of itself 'whirling' has associations far less arcane. It is the action regularly predicated of the great wheel of Fortune. And what more natural, since Fame and Fortune are kin, than that the annex to Fame's palace should share this attribute of Fortune's wheel? It is of this wheel that the *Apocalypsis Goliae* says

> Incedit quilibet cum rota mobili,
> dum mentis volvitur axe volubili
> et circumflectitur voto mutablili
> intus sequitur rotam a simili.   (121–4)

Paintings in manuscripts and murals had made the figure a commonplace long before Chaucer wrote his balades 'de visage sanz peinture'; in the first of which Fortune *whirls* up and down (11)—just as she does in the Chaucerian *Romaunt* (4362; no equivalent in the *Roman de la Rose*); in the (almost equally Chaucerian) *Kingis Quair* (st. 165); in the contemporary alliterative *Morte Arthure* ('abowte cho whirlide a whele with her whitte hondes', 3260)—and in many a Tudor poem. The juxtaposition of Fortune's moving wheel and the hut of wretched straw and gaping roof, representing her reversals, in the miniature reproduced by Patch (op. cit., pl. 7) now takes on a fuller significance.

This rude structure is the fit haunt of half-baked stories, the rumours and travellers' tales that flit in and out of it—raw material on which the poets who gain permanent place in the house of Fame have to work, as different from the finished *opus* as is 'swough' and 'chirking' of the basket-house from the piping and the melody that sounded from the castle walls. By the same token the noise that issues from within the house is not trumpet-toned but like the jarring sound made as a siege-engine hurls its stone (1933–4).

Other differences between the castle and its annex deserve notice:
(i) The shaded side of the hill of ice, the castle's walls, roof, floor thickly plated with gold, its massy pillars, all give the effect of permanence and stability; and we are specifically told that Fame is 'perpetually ystalled' (1364) on her carbuncle throne. The basket house whirls round 'so swift as thought' (1924). The sudden change of tempo

[5] Cf. Roger Sherman Loomis, *Wales and the Arthurian Legend*, Cardiff, 1956, p. 137, and *Arthur of Little Britain*, ed. of 1816, p. 143.

is characteristic of the poem as a whole: against the intellectual excitement of the Prologue has been set the torpor of Morpheus; against the slow movement round the temple of Venus the *prestissimo* of the eagle's descent. (And it is the eagle's lessons on sound laws that we must now recall, for they explain why all noises, all 'tidings', great and small, reach these ever-open doors.)

(ii) Fame's hall is not only spacious but indefinitely expansive (1375, 1494–6). The house of tidings has a measured length of sixty miles— and is crammed to bursting; the visitor can scarcely find room to stand (2041–2); to open one's mouth is to speak into a neighbour's ear (2044–5).

(iii) Fame holds imperial court, has servants at command, and receives profoundest homage. In the house there is no order, no hierarchy, not even a porter. All is constant jostling, plebeian fashion. The throng is noisy, miscellaneous, hurried; shipmen, couriers, pardoners, pilgrims (2120–30). It is like stepping from the decorum of dooms and audiences in the great hall of Westminster to the crowded streets of Thames-side. And Ben Jonson was to localize such a house of fame or report in a London 'shop' where 'all do meet'

> To taste the *cornucopiae* of her rumours,
> Which she, the mother of sport, pleaseth to scatter
> Among the vulgar.
>   (*The Staple of News*, III. ii. 115–20)

(iv) Fame's hall resounds with heavenly melodies sung in her honour (1395 ff.). The house of tidings is 'full of rounings and of jangles' (1960). The discord represents nothing less than the thousand shocks the flesh is heir to. Here is none of the formalized presentation of Fame's suppliants as they wish to be seen, but the raw and random miscellaneity of life, with all its changes and chances. . . .

There remain some miscellaneous, novel, and memorable features of the cage: the 'gigges and chirkinges' (1942–3), the porterless doors, the total absence of ease (1956). They all appear to be suggested by, or rather to suggest—by their very dissimilarity—that other dwell·· ing in a valley, which Chaucer alludes to, otiosely at first sight, in the first book of this poem; namely, the cave of Morpheus. Sleep's house (as Ovid and Chaucer describe it) is the exact antithesis to the abode of 'tidings'. It is doorless, so that there shall be *no* 'chirking' ('there is no door which mai charke', as Gower puts it); and porterless (as well as windowless) for the same reason (*custos in limine nullus*)— whereas in the cage a porter would delay the entrants (1954). Instead of ceaseless activity (1956) there is languorous repose (*muta quies habitat*); instead of 'rouninges and of iangles', not a single sound (*non . . . humanaeve sonum reddunt convicia linguae*). It is the quiet shapes of dreams, not the roof-holes that are there numbered by the thousand (*Met.* xi. 633) and that lie thick 'as leves been on trees' (*Fame,* 1946;

cf. *quot ... silva gerit frondes: Met.* xi. 615). The closing scenes of
the poem are brought by means of such antitheses to stand in ironical
contrast to the opening prayer to the god of sleep and rest. For the
prayer has been answered by a dream that reaches its climax in
scenes of harsh noise and busy clamour.

The re-entry of the eagle into the action at this point likewise serves
to complete the frame of the poem, inasmuch as it recalls the real
purpose of the aerial journey (2007). The bird at once intimates that
the end is near: 'Joves wol thee solace Fynally' (2008–9). Now the
poet can talk to him, and of him, like an old friend; he is *'myn* egle'
now (1900), just as Douglas's interlocutress, after he has passed
through the Palace of Honour, becomes 'my nymph'. But the eagle
at once reminds the poet that he is merely the emissary of Jove, the
deity to whom both Fame and Fortune must be subject. The poet
himself is now openly presented for the first time as a victim of this
Fortune, who

> hath maad amis
> The frot [? *l.* fruit *or* rote] of al thyn hertes reste
> Languisshe and eek in point to breste.   (2016–18)

It is due, then, to the Fortune of whose whirling wheel this cage is
reminiscent, that the poet had served Cupid and Venus 'withoute
guerdoun ever yit' (619). Jove has already offered him partial 'solace'
—by those scenes of *natura naturans* that had led him to cry 'moche
is thy might and thy noblesse'; by the marvels of Fame's palace;
and by the sight of the hardly less wonderful house of twigs. And the
poet has sensed that in this last he may hear 'that leef me were, or that
I wente' (1999). . . .

From *Chaucer's* 'Book of Fame', Clarendon Press, Oxford, 1968,
pp. 165–177.

RAYMOND PRESTON

The *Legend of Good Women*

... If we look through the legends with an eye to what is admirable by the poet's highest standards, we can make, at once, three observations. The first is that he skips over Cleopatra with a momentary interest in an actual sea-fight; second, he finds one or two shivering lines for Piramus and Thisbe; and, third, he is at his best in a passage of the story of Dido. This last is of very much greater interest than his impression of the *Æneid* in the *House of Fame*. It is true that part of the beginning of the legend is another insipid verse abstract; but when he has paid his homage to Virgil, he treats Dido afresh, in a way which is Chaucer and English poetry. In order to enjoy it we have to be aware that this is no competition, but deliberately confined to proportions delicate, sensitive, amusing beside the vast intention of the Latin. The first descriptions of Dido can hardly be referred to Virgil; they are 'conventionally' medieval in diction, and in rhythm Chaucerian. She is seen as a *fresshe lady* capable of love, and not in relation to the politic of Rome or to myth. In the alteration the stature of Virgil's queen is inevitably reduced—but her raging, murderous fury in the *Æneid* is of course outside Chaucer's commission. He has the poetic problem of directing our sympathy towards Dido and against Æneas, and at the same time he has the ironist's consciousness of what he is doing. He assumed that his readers would know, perhaps their Virgil, certainly their *Romance of the Rose*, in which the story is told by La Vieille to show that in the opinion of the decrepit quean One Lover is Not Enough. He keeps at a distance from the deities who produce epic crises—

> I can nat seyn if that hit be possible,
> But Venus hadde him maked invisible—
> thus seith the book . . .[1]

—and makes no miraculous apparition of Æneas in celestial splendour; only the bare statement,

> Unto the quene appeared Eneas,
> And openly biknew that it was he.[2]

Where Virgil's hero appears radiant from the circling cloud, Chaucer

[1] 1020–2
[2] 1057–8
Biknew confessed

makes a note of the facial muscles and skull formation, as dispassionately as if he were observing the Miller—

> . . . he was lyk a knyght,
> And suffisaunt of persone and of myght,
> And lyk to been a verray gentil man;
> And wel his wordes he besette can,
> And hadde a noble visage for the nones,
> And formed wel of braunes and of bones.[3]

—and then adds, without great conviction,

> For after Venus hadde he swich fayrnesse
> That no man myghte be half so fayr, I gesse.

Thus he plays his game of carrying out instructions of the court of love.

The two outstanding passages of poetry show the action of Eros: first in the munificence of Dido, which Chaucer, passing over the golden splendour of the feast, develops in his own way:

> To daunsynge chaumbers ful of paramentes,
> Of riche beddes, and of ornementes,
> This Eneas is led, after the mete.
> And with the quene whan that he hadde sete,
> And spices parted, and the wyn agon,
> Unto his chambres was he led anon . . .
> There nas courser wel ybrydeled non,
> Ne stede, for the justing wel to gon,
> Ne large palfrey, esy for the nones,
> Ne jewel, fretted ful of ryche stones,
> Ne sakkes ful of gold, of large wyghte,
> Ne ruby non, that shynede by nyghte,
> Ne gentil hautein faucoun heroner,
> Ne hound, for hert or wilde bor or der,
> Ne coupe of gold, with floreyns newe ybete,
> That in the land of Libie may be gete,
> That Dido ne hath it Eneas ysent;
> And al is payed, what that he hath spent.[4]

So Dido is expressed through her gifts, with a vitality that reaches a point of aristocratic excellence in the line *Ne gentil hautein faucoun heroner.* This quality is still clearer in the finest passage of the legends,

---

[3] 1066–71
Besette employ
   Compare the Canterbury *Prologue* A 545–6, quoted below, p. 174, together with a parallel couplet from the popular romance *Ipomydon*. I do not think we need assume that Chaucer misunderstood *Os humerosque deo similis* (*Æneid* I 589).
[4] 1106–25
Paramentes rich hangings   *Sete* sat   *Wyghte* weight
Hautein proud   *Heroner* for herons

Chaucer's handling of *Oceanum interea surgens Aurora reliquit* . . .

> The dawenyng up-rist out of the see:
> This amorous queen chargeth hire meynee
> The nettes dresse, and speres brode and kene;
> An huntyng wol this lusty freshe queene,
> So priketh hire this newe joly wo.
> To hors is al hir lusty folk ygo;
> Into the court the houndes been ybrought;
> And upon coursers, swift as any thought,
> Hire yonge knyghtes hoven al aboute,
> And of hire women ek an huge route.
> Upon a thikke palfrey, paper-whit,
> With sadel red, enbrouded with delyt,
> Of gold the barres up-enbossed hye,
> Sit Dido, al in gold and perre wrye;
> And she as fair as is the bryghte morwe,
> That heleth syke folk of nyghtes sorwe.[5]

In Virgil it is the queen who lingers, not the princes of Carthage; and her *sonipes* here becomes a *thikke palfrey, paper-whit*. Chaucer's last couplet, with its beautiful double rhyme, and its imagery in the troubadour tradition, is his own—and so, in effect, is the whole passage.

What is positive in this comes of a natural impulse renewing life, creative as in the Spring movement of the Canterbury *Prologue*. The sensitive physical excitement of the scene is in the mettle of Æneas's horse, set off by the virility of *these yonge folk*.

> Upon a courser stertlynge as the fyr—
> Men myghte turne hym with a litel wyr—
> Sit Eneas, lik Phebus to devyse,
> So was he fressh arayed in his wyse.
> The fomy brydel with the bit of gold
> Governeth he, ryght as himself hath wold.
> And forth this noble queen thus lat I ride
> On huntynge, with this Troyan by hyre side.
>   The herde of hertes founden is anon,
> With 'hey! go bet! pryke thow! lat gon, lat gon!
> Why nyl the leoun comen, or the bere,
> That I myghte ones mete hym with this spere?'
> Thus seye these yonge folk, and up they kylle
> These bestes wilde, and han hem at here wille.[6]

When they are surprised by the thunderstorm,

> She fledde hireself into a litel cave,
> And with hire wente this Eneas also.

[5] 1188–203
Meynee retinue   *Hoven* hover   *Thikke* stout   *Perre* precious stones   *Wrye* covered
[6] 1204–17
Stertlynge as the fyr leaping like flame   *Wyr* bit   *Wold* wished

I not, with hem if there wente any mo;
The autour maketh of it no mencioun.[7]

Chaucer can smile without suspicion of archness: he has done his job
admirably.

The tragic conflict in Virgil's Dido, between the new desire and the
old duty, must not of course be attempted; and certain passages remain
to be smoothed over.

> *. . . neque enim specie famave movetur*
> *Nec iam furtivum Dido meditatur amorem;*
> *Coniugium vocat; hoc prætexit nomine culpam.*
> > *Æneid*

> For there hath Eneas ykneled so,
> And told hire al his herte and al his wo,
> And swore so depe to hire to be trewe,
> For wel or wo, and chaunge hire for no newe,
> And as a fals lovere so wel can pleyne,
> That sely Dido rewede on his peyne,
> And tok hym for husbonde, and becom his wyf
> For evermo, whil that hem laste lyf.[8]
> > *Legenda Didonis Martiris*

It is as if Chaucer translated Virgil's *enim*, and then saw that the rest
simply would not do. And so, soon after this, he may plead for Good
Women:

> O sely wemen, ful of innocence,
> Ful of pite, of trouthe, and conscience,
> What maketh yow to men to truste so?
> Have ye swych routhe upon hyre feyned wo,
> And han swich olde ensaumples yow beforn?
> Se ye nat alle how they ben foresworn?
> Where sen ye oon, that he ne hath laft his leef,
> Or ben unkynde, or don hire som myscheef,
> Or piled hire, or bosted of his dede?
> Ye may as wel it sen, as ye may rede.
> Tak hede now of this grete gentil-man,
> This Troyan, that so wel hire plesen can,
> That feyneth hym so trewe and obeysynge,
> So gentil, and so privy of his doinge,
> And can so wel don alle his obeysaunces
> And wayten hire at festes and at daunces

[7] 1225–8
Not do not know
  [8] *Æneid* IV 170–3: thus translated by Dryden:
> The queen, whom sense of honour could not move,
> No longer made a secret of her love,
> But called it marriage; by that specious name
> To veil the crime and sanctify the shame.
Legend of Good Women 1232–9
Sely innocent

And whan she goth to temple and hom ageyn
And fasten til he hath his lady seyn
And beren in his devyses, for hire sake,
Not I not what; and songes wolde he make,
Justen, and don of armes many thynges,
Sende hire lettres, tokens, broches, rynges—
Now herkneth how he shal his lady serve! . . .[9]

This is entirely medieval; and the ironical reserve is Chaucer's. For the moment he is like an actor trying very hard to be out of breath, and succeeding.

At the end of the poem, the furious majesty of Virgil's queen is changed to Chaucerian pathos and grace:

She axeth hym anon what hym myslyketh—
'My dere herte, which that I love most?'
    'Certes', quod he, 'this nyght my faderes gost
Hath in my slep so sore me tormented,
And ek Mercurie his message hath presented,
That nedes to the conquest of Ytayle
My destine is sone for to sayle;
For which, me thynketh, brosten is myn herte!'
Therwith his false teres out they sterte;
And taketh hire withinne his armes two.
    'Is this in ernest?' quod she, 'wole ye so?
Have ye nat sworn to wyve me to take?
Allas! what woman wole ye of me make?
I am a gentile woman and a queen.
Ye wole nat from youre wif thus foule fleen?
That I was born, allas? What shal I do?'
    To telle in short, this noble quen Dydo,
She seketh halwes and doth sacryfise;
She kneleth, cryeth, that routhe is to devyse;
Conjureth hym, and profereth hym to be
His thral, his servant in the leste degre;
She falleth hym to fote and swouneth ther,
Dischevele, with hire bryghte gilte her . . .'[10]

Perhaps there is something here, even if it is only a line, which is not entirely obliterated by the nightmare and the horror in the *Æneid*.

This music is successful with a 'dying fall': let him steal Ovid's *albus olor* for the purpose—

'Ryght so', quod she, 'as that the white swan
Ayens his deth begynnyth for to synge,
Right so to yow make I my compleynynge.

[9] 1254–76
Leef beloved   *Piled* despoiled   *And beren in his devyses* . . . carry
I do not know what tokens in his heraldic decoration.
[10] 1293–315
Halwes shrines

Not that I trowe to geten yow ageyn,
For wel I wot that it is al in veyn,
Syn that the goddes been contraire to me.
But syn my name is lost through yow,' quod she,
'I may wel lese a word on yow, or letter,
Al be it that I shal ben nevere the better;
For thilke wynd that blew you're ship awey,
The same wynd hath blowe awey youre fey.'[11]

The white swan had already sung in Anelida's *compleynt*, but in these closing couplets she has a new voice . . .

Towards the beginning of my last chapter I spoke of the 'fresh verse-form' of the prologue to the *Legend of Good Women*, but without mentioning the probability, long ago argued by Professor Lowes, that Chaucer had previously conducted his experiments in many of the legends themselves. Their duller tracts are so often reminiscent of the wicked knight in *Anelida and Arcite* that until decisive evidence turns up no more need be said. The stories, whenever they were written, remain unequal; remove the dust, and a few passages look very well in daylight. They are certainly not *satire* against women, or even inverted satire. What they are, Lydgate knew:

> This poete wrote at Request of the quene
> A Legende of parfight hoolynesse
> Off goode women to Fynden out nyntene
> That did excelle in bounte and fayrnesse,
> But for his labour and his besynesse
>> Was inportable his wittes to encoumbre
>> In al this world to Fynde so greet a noumbre . . .
> . . . Redith the legende of martyrs of Cupide
> Which that Chaucer in Ordre as they stood,
> Compyled of women that wer callyd good.[12]

This, in spite of Lydgate's reputation, is not humourless; and poets, in their verse, may be critics of other poets in other ways. They may also be critics of themselves. We have the first form of criticism in the legends, and the second in their prologue. This critical activity will not alone make a masterly poem, though it is a condition of any fruitful experiment or poetic advance. The greater progress here is underground, showing itself, now and again, in new achievement of rhythm and imagery. Chaucer can sing praises—

> Glorye and honour, Virgil Mantuan,
> Be to thy name!

—and arrange to look smaller than he really is behind a pre-eminent classical master. On the other hand, the *Legend of Good Women*, or a

---

[11] V 5974–97
[12] Prologue to Book I of the *Fall of Princes*
For his labour . . . he was driven near to distraction for his pains

great deal of it, may be read as criticism of Ovid, even if rather more than has so far been proved is closer to a French or Italian version of the Latin. It would be difficult to find in English a more exquisite homage to the *Heroides* than Dido's letter, or the conclusion of the legend of Ariadne: and at the same time no Englishman of Chaucer's sense would pass a simile which distracts attention to faulty plumbing in a Roman bathroom.[13] Professor Shannon tells us that Chaucer had chosen the best of Ovid's stories by the time he abandoned the *Legend*, and had learnt the art of brief narrative in the process. The poet of Criseyde, bringing Ovid and classical story into English, could have found nowhere else a complete analysis of female emotion: refined and sophisticated, and fitting the ladies of the court.[14] But —and this is the criticism—his poetry at the beginning of the legend of Philomela, upon Tereus and God the giver of forms, is also a comment on Ovid's relish of horrors that still have power to corrupt. There is no farcical engagement, here, with the naughty male. Chaucer is propounding a serious problem: the problem of evil. As for Good Women, Ovid would have told him that they knew too little (poor dears) of either the Art of Love or its Remedies.

From *Chaucer*, Sheed and Ward, 1952, pp. 129–145.

---

[13] *Metamorphoses* IV 121–4: altered in *Legend of Good Women* 851–2.
[14] Edgar Finley Shannon, *Chaucer and the Roman Poets*, Harvard University Press, 1929, O.U.P., pp. 168, 176, 300.

C. S. LEWIS

What Chaucer really did to
Il Filostrato

... The majority of his modifications are corrections of errors which Boccaccio had committed against the code of courtly love; and modifications of this kind have not been entirely neglected by criticism. It has not, however, been sufficiently observed that these are only part and parcel of a general process of medievalization. They are, indeed, the most instructive part of that process, and even in the present discussion must claim the chief place; but in order to restore them to their proper setting it will be convenient to make a division of the different capacities in which Chaucer approached his original. These will, of course, be found to overlap in the concrete; but that is no reason for not plucking them ideally apart in the interests of clarity.

I. Chaucer approached his work as an 'Historial' poet contributing to the story of Troy. I do not mean that he necessarily believed his tale to be wholly or partly a record of fact, but his attitude towards it in this respect is different from Boccaccio's. Boccaccio, we may surmise, wrote for an audience who were beginning to look at poetry in our own way. For them *Il Filostrato* was mainly, though not entirely, 'a new poem by Boccaccio'. Chaucer wrote for an audience who still looked at poetry in the medieval fashion—a fashion for which the real literary units were 'matters', 'stories', and the like, rather than individual authors. For them the *Book of Troilus* was partly, though of course only partly, 'a new bit of the Troy story', or even 'a new bit of the matter of Rome'. Hence Chaucer expects them to be interested not only in the personal drama between his little group of characters but in that whole world of story which makes this drama's context: like children looking at a landscape picture and wanting to know what happens to the road after it disappears into the frame. For the same reason they will want to know his authorities. Passages in which Chaucer has departed from his original to meet this demand will easily occur to the memory. Thus, in i. 141 et seq., he excuses himself for not telling us more about the military history of the Trojan war, and adds what is almost a footnote to tell his audience where they can find that missing part of the story—'in Omer, or in Dares, or in Dyte'. Boccaccio had merely sketched in, in the preceding stanza, a general picture of war sufficient to provide the background for his own story —much as a dramatist might put *Alarums within* in a stage direction:

he has in view an audience fully conscious that all this is mere necessary 'setting' or hypothesis. Thus again, in iv. 120 et seq., Chaucer
inserts into the speech of *Calkas* an account of the quarrel between
Phebus and *Neptunus* and *Lameadoun*. This is not dramatically necessary. All that was needed for *Calkas's* argument has already been given
in lines 111 and 112 (cf. *Filostrato*, IV. xi). The Greek leaders did not
need to be told about Laomedon; but Chaucer is not thinking of the
Greek leaders; he is thinking of his audience who will gladly learn, or be
reminded, of that part of the cycle. At lines 204 et seq. he inserts a
note on the later history of *Antenor* for the same reason. In the fifth
book he inserts unnecessarily lines 1464–1510 from the story of
Thebes. The spirit in which this is done is aptly expressed in his own
words:

> And so descendeth down from gestes olde
> To Diomede.   (v. 1511, 1512)

The whole 'matter of Rome' is still a unity, with a structure and life
of its own. That part of it which the poem in hand is treating, which is,
so to speak, in focus, must be seen fading gradually away into its
'historial' surroundings. The method is the antithesis of that which
produces the 'framed' story of a modern writer: it is a method which
romance largely took over from the epic.

II.   Chaucer approached his work as a pupil of the rhetoricians
and a firm believer in the good, old, and now neglected maxim of
Dante: *omnis qui versificatur suos versus exornare debet in quantum
potest*. This side of Chaucer's poetry has been illustrated by Mr
Manly[1] so well that most readers will not now be in danger of neglect-
ing it. A detailed application of this new study to the *Book of Troilus*
would here detain us too long, but a cursory glance shows that Chaucer
found his original too short and proceeded in many places to 'amplify'
it. He began by abandoning the device—that of invoking his lady
instead of the Muses—whereby Boccaccio had given a lyrical instead
of a rhetorical turn to the invocation, and substituted an address to
Thesiphone (*Filostrato*, I. i–v, cf. *Troilus*, i. 1–14). He added at the
beginning of his second book an invocation of *Cleo* and an apology
of the usual medieval type, for the defects of his work (ii. 15–21).
Almost immediately afterwards he inserted a *descriptio* of the month
of May (an innovation which concerned him as poet of courtly love
no less than as rhetorician) which is extremely beautiful and appropriate, but which follows, none the less, conventional lines. The season
is fixed by astronomical references, and *Proigne* and *Tereus* appear
just where we should expect them (ii. 50–6, 64–70). In the third book
the scene of the morning parting between the two lovers affords a
complicated example of Chaucer's medievalization. In his original
(III. xlii) Chaucer read

[1] *Chaucer and the Rhetoricians*, Wharton Lecture XVII, 1926.

> Ma poich' e galli presso al giorno udiro
> Cantar per l'aurora che surgea.

He proceeded to amplify this, first by the device of *Circuitio* or *Circumlocutio*; *galli*, with the aid of Alanus de Insulis, became 'the cok, comune astrologer'. Not content with this, he then repeated the sense of that whole phrase by the device *Expolitio*, of which the formula is *Multiplice forma Dissimuletur idem: varius sis et tamen idem*,[2] and the theme 'Dawn came' is varied with *Lucifer* and *Fortuna Minor*, till it fills a whole stanza (iii. 1415–21). In the next stanza of Boccaccio he found a short speech by *Griseida*, expressing her sorrow at the parting which dawn necessitated: but this was not enough for him. As poet of love he wanted his *alba*; as rhetorician he wanted his *apostropha*. He therefore inserted sixteen lines of address to Night (1427–42), during which he secured the additional advantage, from the medieval point of view, of 'som doctryne' (1429–32). In lines 1452–70 he inserted antiphonally Troilus's *alba*, for which the only basis in Boccaccio was the line *Il giorno che venia maledicendo* (III. xliv). The passage is an object lesson for those who tend to identify the traditional with the dull. Its matter goes back to the ancient sources of medieval love poetry, notably to Ovid, *Amores*, i. 13, and it has been handled often before, and better handled, by the Provençals. Yet it is responsible for one of the most vivid and beautiful expressions that Chaucer ever used.

> Accursed be thy coming into Troye
> For every bore hath oon of thy bright eyen.

A detailed study of the *Book of Troilus* would reveal this 'rhetoricization', if I may coin an ugly word, as the common quality of many of Chaucer's additions. As examples of *Apostropha* alone I may mention, before leaving this part of the subject, iii. 301 et seq. (*O tonge*), 617 et seq. (*But o Fortune*), 715 et seq. (*O Venus*), and 813 et seq. where Chaucer is following Boethius.

III.   Chaucer approached his work as a poet of *doctryne* and sentence. This is a side of his literary character which twentieth-century fashions encourage us to overlook, but, of course, no honest historian can deny it. His contemporaries and immediate successors did not. His own creatures, the pilgrims, regarded *mirthe* and *doctryne*,[3] or, as it is elsewhere expressed, *sentence* and *solas*,[4] as the two alternative, and equally welcome, excellences of a story. In the same spirit Hoccleve praises Chaucer as the *mirour of fructuous entendement* and the universal *fadir in science*[5]—a passage, by the by, to be recommended to those who are astonished that the fifteenth century should

---

[2] Geoffroi de Vinsauf, *Poetr. Nov*, 220–5.
[3] *Canterbury Tales*, B 2125.
[4] Ibid., A 798.
[5] *Regement*, 1963 et seq.

imitate those elements of Chaucer's genius which it enjoyed instead of those which we enjoy. In respect of *doctryne*, then, Chaucer found his original deficient, and *amended* it. The example which will leap to everyone's mind is the Boethian discussion on free will (iv. 946–1078). To Boccaccio, I suspect, this would have seemed as much an excrescence as it does to the modern reader; to the unjaded appetites of Chaucer's audience mere thickness in a wad of manuscript was a merit. If the author was so 'courteous beyond covenant' as to give you an extra bit of *doctryne* (or of story), who would be so churlish as to refuse it on the pedantic ground of irrelevance? . . .

IV.   Finally, Chaucer approached his work as the poet of courtly love. He not only modified his story so as to make it a more accurate representation in action of the orthodox erotic code, but he also went out of his way to emphasize its didactic element. Andreas Capellanus had given instructions to lovers; Guillaume de Lorris had given instructions veiled and decorated by allegory; Chaucer carries the process a stage further and gives instruction by example in the course of a concrete story. But he does not forget the instructional side of his work. In the following paragraphs I shall sometimes quote parallels to Chaucer's innovations from the earlier love literature, but it must not be thought that I suppose my quotations to represent Chaucer's immediate source.

1.   Boccaccio in his induction, after invoking his mistress instead of the Muses, inserts (i. vi) a short request for lovers in general that they will pray for him. The prayer itself is disposed of in a single line.

> Per me vi prego ch'amore preghiate.

This is little more than a conceit, abandoned as soon as it is used: a modern poet could almost do the like. Chaucer devotes four stanzas (i. 22–49) to this prayer. If we make an abstract of both passages, Boccaccio will run 'Pray for me to Love', while Chaucer will run 'Remember, all lovers, your old unhappiness, and pray, for the unsuccessful, that they may come to solace; for me, that I may be enabled to tell this story; for those in despair, that they may die; for the fortunate, that they may persevere, and please their ladies in such manner as may advance the glory of Love'. The important point here is not so much that Chaucer expands his original, as that he renders it more liturgical: his prayer, with its careful discriminations in inter-cession for the various recognized stages of the amorous life, and its final reference *ad Amoris majorem gloriam*, is a collect. Chaucer is emphasizing that parody, or imitation, or rivalry—I know not which to call it—of the Christian religion which was inherent in traditional *Frauendienst*. The thing can be traced back to Ovid's purely ironical worship of Venus and Amor in the *De Arte Amatoria*. The idea of a love religion is taken up and worked out, though still with equal flip-pancy, in terms of medieval Christianity, by the twelfth-century

F

poet of the *Concilium Romaricimontis*,[6] where Love is given Cardinals (female), the power of visitation, and the power of cursing. Andreas Capellanus carried the process a stage further and gave Love the power of distributing reward and punishment after death. But while his hell of cruel beauties (*Siccitas*), his purgatory of beauties promiscuously kind (*Humiditas*), and his heaven of true lovers (*Amoenitas*)[7] can hardly be other than playful, Andreas deals with the love religion much more seriously than the author of the *Concilium*. The lover's qualification is *morum probitas*: he must be truthful and modest, a good Catholic, clean in his speech, hospitable, and ready to return good for evil. There is nothing in *saeculo bonum* which is not derived from love:[8] it may even be said in virtue of its severe standard of constancy, to be 'a kind of chastity'—*reddit hominem castitatis quasi virtute decoratum.*[9]

In all this we are far removed from the tittering nuns and *clerici* of the *Concilium*. In Chrestien, the scene in which Lancelot keels and adores the bed of Guinevere (as if before a *corseynt*)[10] is, I think, certainly intended to be read seriously: what mental reservations the poet himself had on the whole business is another question. In Dante the love religion has become wholly and unequivocally serious by fusing with the real religion: the distance between the *Amor deus omnium quotquot sunt amantium* of the *Concilium*, and the *segnore di pauroso aspetto* of the *Vita Nuova*,[11] is the measure of the tradition's real flexibility and universality. It is this quasi-religious element in the content, and this liturgical element in the diction, which Chaucer found lacking in his original at the very opening of the book, and which he supplied. The line

> That Love hem bringe in hevene to solas

is particularly instructive.

2. In the Temple scene (Chaucer, i. 155–315. *Filostrato*, I. xix-xxxii) Chaucer found a stanza which it was very necessary to *reducen*. It was Boccaccio's twenty-third, in which Troilus, after indulging in his 'cooling card for lovers', mentions that he has himself been singed with that fire, and even hints that he has had his successes; but the pleasures were not worth the pains. The whole passage is a typical example of that Latin spirit which in all ages (except perhaps our own) has made Englishmen a little uncomfortable; the hero must be a lady-killer from the very beginning, or the audience will think him a milksop and a booby. To have abashed, however temporarily, these

---

[6] *Zeitschrift für Deutsches Alterthum*, vii, pp. 160 et seq.

[7] Andreas Capellanus, *De Arte Honeste Amandi*, ed. Troejel, i. 6 D² (pp. 91–108).

[8] Ibid., i. 6 A (p. 28).

[9] *Lancelot*, 4670, 4734 et seq.

[10] Ibid., i. 4 (p. 10).

[11] *Vit. Nuov.* iii.

strutting Latinisms, is not least among the virtues of medieval *Frauendienst*: and for Chaucer as its poet, this stanza was emphatically one of those that 'would never do'. He drops it quietly out of its place, and thus brings the course of his story nearer to that of the *Romance of the Rose*. The parallelism is so far intact. Troilus, an unattached young member of the courtly world, wandering idly about the Temple, is smitten with Love. In the same way the Dreamer having been admitted by Ydelnesse into the garden goes 'Pleying along ful merily'[12] until he looks in the fatal well. If he had already met Love outside the garden the whole allegory would have to be reconstructed.

3. A few lines lower Chaucer found in his original the words

> il quale amor trafisse
> Più ch'alcun altro, pria del tempio uscisse.   (I. xxv)

Amor trafisse in Boccaccio is hardly more than a literary variant for 'he fell in love': the allegory has shrunk into a metaphor and even that metaphor is almost unconscious and fossilized. Over such a passage one can imagine Chaucer exclaiming, *tantamne rem tam negligenter?* He at once goes back through the metaphor to the allegory that begot it, and gives us his own thirtieth stanza (i. 204–10) on the god of Love in anger bending his bow. The image is very ancient and goes back at least as far as Apollonius Rhodius.[13] Ovid was probably the intermediary who conveyed it to the Middle Ages. Chrestien uses it, with particular emphasis on Love as the avenger of contempt.[14] But Chaucer need not have gone further to find it than to the *Romance of the Rose*:[15] with which, here again, he brings his story into line.

4. But even this was not enough. Boccaccio's *Amor trafisse* had occurred in a stanza where the author apostrophizes the *Cecità delle mondane menti*, and reflects on the familiar contrast between human expectations and the actual course of events. But this general contrast seemed weak to the poet of courtly love: what he wanted was the explicit erotic *moral*, based on the special contrast between the ὕβρις of the young scoffer and the complete surrender which the offended deity soon afterwards extracted from him. This conception, again, owes much to Ovid; but between Ovid and the Middle Ages comes the later practice of the ancient Epithalamium during the decline of antiquity and the Dark Ages: to which, as I hope to show elsewhere, the system of courtly love as a whole is heavily indebted. Thus in the fifth century Sidonius Apollinarus in an Epithalamium, makes the bridegroom just such another as Troilus: a proud scoffer humbled by Love. Amor brings to Venus the triumphant news

---

12 *R. R.* 1329 (English Version).
13 *Argonaut*, iii. 275 et seq.
14 *Cligès*, 460; cf. 770.
15 *R. R.* 1330 et seq.; 1715 et seq.

> Nova gaudia porto
> Felicis praedae, genetrix. Calet ille *superbus*
> Ruricius.[16]

Venus replies

> gaudemus nate, *rebellem*
> Quod vincis.

In a much stronger poem, by the Bishop Ennodius, it is not the $\ddot{v}\beta\rho\iota\varsigma$ of a single youth, but of the world, that has stung the deities of love into retributive action. Cupid and Venus are introduced deploring the present state of Europe

> Frigida consumens multorum possidet artus
> Virginitas.[17]

and Venus meets the situation by a threat that she'll 'larn 'em':

> Discant populi tunc crescere divam
> Cum neglecta iacet.[18]

They conclude by attacking one Maximus and thus bringing about the marriage which the poem was written to celebrate. Venantius Fortunatus, in his Epithalamium for Brunchild reproduces, together with Ennodius's spring morning, Ennodius's boastful Cupid, and makes the god, after an exhibitiion of his archery, announce to his mother, *mihi vincitur alter Achilles*.[19] In Chrestien the rôle of tamed rebel is transferred to the woman. In *Cligès* Soredamors confesses that Love has humbled her pride by force, and doubts whether such extorted service will find favour.[20] In strict obedience to this tradition Chaucer inserts his lines 214–31, emphasizing the dangers of $\ddot{v}\beta\rho\iota\varsigma$ against Love and the certainty of its ultimate failure; and we may be thankful that he did, since it gives us the lively and touching simile of *proude Bayard*. Then, mindful of his instructional purpose, he adds four stanzas more (239–66), in which he directly exhorts his readers to avoid the error of Troilus, and that for two reasons: firstly, because Love *cannot* be resisted (this is the policeman's argument—we may as well 'come quiet'); and secondly, because Love is a thing 'so vertuous in kinde'. The second argument, of course, follows traditional lines, and recalls Andreas's theory of Love as the source of all secular virtue.

5. In lines 330–50 Chaucer again returns to Troilus's scoffing—a scoffing this time assumed as a disguise. I do not wish to press the possibility that Chaucer in this passage is attempting, in virtue of his instructional purpose, to stress the lover's virtue of secrecy more than he found it stressed in his original; for Boccaccio, probably for

[16] *Sid. Apoll.* Carm. xi. 61.
[17] Ennodius Carm. I, iv. 57.
[18] Ibid. 84.
[19] Venant. Fort. VI, i.
[20] *Cligès*, 682, 241.

different reasons, does not leave that side of the subject untouched. But it is interesting to note a difference in the content between this scoffing and that of Boccaccio (*Filostrato* I. xxi, xxii). Boccaccio's is based on contempt for women, fickle as wind, and heartless. Chaucer's is based on the hardships of love's *lay* or religion: hardships arising from the uncertainty of the most orthodox *observances*, which may lead to various kinds of harm and may be taken amiss by the lady. Boccaccio dethrones the deity: Chaucer complains of the severity of the cult. It is the difference between an atheist and a man who humorously insists that he 'is not of religioun'.

6. In the first dialogue between Troilus and Pandarus the difference between Chaucer and his original can best be shown by an abstract. Boccaccio (II. vi–xxviii) would run roughly as follows:

T. Well, if you must know, I am in love. But don't ask me with whom (vi–viii).

P. Why did you not tell me long ago? I could have helped you (ix).

T. What use would *you* be? Your own suit never succeeded (ix).

P. A man can often guide others better than himself (x).

T. I can't tell you, because it is a relation of yours (xv).

P. A fig for relations! Who is it? (xvi).

T. (after a pause) Griseida.

P. Splendid! Love has fixed your heart in a good place. She is an admirable person. The only trouble is that she is rather *pie* (*onesta*): but I'll soon see to that (xxiii). Every woman is amorous at heart: they are only anxious to save their reputations (xxvii). I'll do all I can for you (xxviii).

Chaucer (i. 603–1008) would be more like this:

T. Well, if you must know, I am in love. But don't ask me with whom (603–16).

P. Why did you not tell me long ago? I could have helped you (617–20).

T. What use would *you* be? Your own suit never succeeded (621–3).

P. A man can often guide others better than himself, as we see from the analogy of the whetstone. Remember the doctrine of contraries, and what Oenone said. As regards secrecy, remember that all virtue is a mean between two extremes (624–700).

T. Do leave me alone (760).

P. If you die, how will she interpret it? Many lovers have served for twenty years without a single kiss. But should they despair? No, they should think it a guerdon even to serve (761–819).

T. (much moved by this argument, 820–6) What shall I do? Fortune is my foe (827–40).

P. Her wheel is always turning. Tell me who your mistress is. If it were my sister, you should have her (841–61).

T. (after a pause)—My sweet foe is Criseyde (870–5).

P. Splendid: Love has fixed your heart in a good place. This ought to gladden you, firstly, because to love such a lady is nothing but good: secondly, because if she has all these virtues, she

must have Pity too. You are very fortunate that Love has
treated you so well, considering your previous scorn of him.
You must repent at once (874-935).
T. (kneeling) Mea Culpa! (936-8).
P. Good. All will now come right. Govern yourself properly: you
know that a divided heart can have no grace. I have reasons
for being hopeful. No man or woman was ever born who was
not apt for love, either natural or celestial: and celestial love
is not fitted to Criseyde's years. I will do all I can for you.
Love converted you of his goodness. Now that you are converted, you will be as conspicuous among his saints as you
formerly were among the sinners against him (939-1008).

In this passage it is safe to say that every single alteration by Chaucer
is an alteration in the direction of medievalism. The Whetstone,
Oenone, Fortune, and the like we have already discussed: the signific-
ance of the remaining innovations may now be briefly indicated. In
Boccaccio the reason for Troilus's hesitation in giving the name is
Criseida's relationship to Pandaro: and like a flash comes back
Pandaro's startling answer. In Chaucer his hesitation is due to the
courtly lover's certainty that 'she nil to noon suich wrecche as I be
wonne' (778) and that 'full harde it wer to helpen in this cas' (836).
Pandaro's original

> Se quella ch'ami fosse mia sorella
> A mio potere avrai tuo piacer d'ella   (xvi)

is reproduced in the English, but by removing the words that provoked
it in the Italian (E tua parenta, xv) Chaucer makes it merely a general
protestation of boundless friendship in love, instead of a cynical
defiance of scruples already raised (Chaucer 861). Boccaccio had
delighted to bring the purities of family life and the profligacy of his
young man about town into collision, and to show the triumph of
the latter. Chaucer keeps all the time within the charmed circle of
Frauendienst and allows no conflict but that of the lover's hopes and
fears. Again, Boccaccio's Pandaro has no argument to use against
Troilo's silence, but the argument 'I may help you'. Chaucer's
Pandarus, on finding that this argument fails, proceeds to expound
the code. The fear of dishonour in the lady's eyes, the duty of humble
but not despairing service in the face of all discouragement, and the
acceptance of this service as its own reward, form the substance of six
stanzas in the English text (lines 768-819): at least, if we accept
four lines very characteristically devoted to 'Ticius' and what 'bokes
telle' of him. Even more remarkable is the difference between the
behaviour of the two Pandars after the lady's name has been disclosed.
Boccaccio's, cynical as ever, encourages Troilo by the reflection that
female virtue is not really a serious obstacle: Chaucer's makes the
virtue of the lady itself the ground for hope—arguing scholastically
that the *genus* of virtue implies that *species* thereof which is *Pitee*

897–900). In what follows, Pandarus, while continuing to advise, becomes an adviser of a slightly dierent sort. He instructs Troilus not so much on his relationship to the Lady as on his relationship to Love. He endeavours to awaken in Troilus a devout sense of his previous sins against that deity (904–30) and is not satisfied without confession (931–8), briefly enumerates the commandments (953–9), and warns his penitent of the dangers of a divided heart.

In establishing such a case as mine, the author who transfers relentlessly to his article all the passages listed in his private notes can expect nothing but weariness from the reader. If I am criticized, I am prepared to produce for my contention many more evidential passages of the same kind. I am prepared to show how many of the beauties introduced by Chaucer, such as the song of Antigone or the riding past of Troilus, are introduced to explain and mitigate and delay the surrender of the heroine, who showed in Boccaccio a facility condemned by the courtly code.[21] I am prepared to show how Chaucer never forgets his erotically didactic purpose; and how, anticipating criticism as a teacher of love, he guards himself by reminding us that

> For to winne love in sondry ages
> In sondry londes, sondry ben usages.[22]   (ii. 27)

But the reader whose stomach is limited would be tired, and he who is interested may safely be left to follow the clue for himself. . . .

From 'What Chaucer really did to *Il Filostrato*', *Essays and Studies*, Vol. XVII, 1932, pp. 56–74.

---

[21] A particularly instructive comparison could be drawn between the Chaucerian Cresseide's determination to yield, yet to seem to yield by force and deception, and Bialacoil's behaviour. *R. R.* 12607–88: specially 12682, 3.
[22] Cf. ii. 1023 et seq.

G. T. SHEPHERD

The Narrator in *Troilus and Criseyde*

... Although the story is told in terms of historical conventions about love and war which can perhaps be broadly identified, the *sens* of this poem was never simple and consistent, to be absorbed unconsciously in large measure. The view we are required to take of the *sens* as well as of the matter is being constantly altered and manipulated. The telling demands that we change our filter repeatedly and the changes seem to be quite deliberately devised. In the poem the signals of change are given by the Narrator. In the original telling of the poem they were probably actually worked by the reciter of the poem.

It could be claimed that the Narrator is the only fully-developed character in the poem—he is certainly the only figure who reacts and changes with the sequence of the events narrated. The Narrator is an I, a mask worn by the person who speaks the script. This public apparition of an I is not, of course, Chaucer the man, not even Chaucer the poet: it is the mask made by Chaucer, originally perhaps, as the frontispiece to the Corpus *Troilus* Manuscript suggests, for Chaucer the performer to wear as he delivered the poem to a court audience. The I is not then the voice of the 'second author', as this apparition is sometimes called in dealing with a modern novel: it is rather the voice of a 'third speaker'. As long as a printed text is thought of as the standard form of a story, the recession of speakers is difficult to grasp. Chaucer certainly aspired to give *Troilus and Criseyde* a fixed text and said so quite plainly at the end of the poem. But the norm of composition for a vernacular poet was still the actual speaking of the story, the *narratio*. In composing *Troilus and Criseyde* before delivery, Chaucer was doing what an established comedian of stage or screen who is his own script-writer does in preparing one of his entertainments. He has to subdue his selected matter to his own technique of delivery, to exploit the reputation he has already acquired and the responses he should be able to anticipate from a particular and fairly familiar audience. He has to make a script which shall suit his story, his public appearance and the audience. He knows that the recognized features of the mask he is to wear will modify and be modified by the story. For the mask mediates the story. The entertainer is the manipulator and also part of the story he is presenting.

Similarly, the Narrator in *Troilus and Criseyde* is both inside and outside the story. Introducing the poem the Narrator speaks about himself. Later, at points of the story he will act the part of Troilus or Pandarus or Criseyde, and project to his audience a degree of identification. Sometimes he will speak as if he were the unobtrusive and rapid recorder of events. Sometimes, the Narrator delivers, in his own assumed first person as *auctor*, appropriate didactic comment. Sometimes he is on intimate and knowledgeable terms with the audience, and distances his story material. He exhibits a whole range of devices by which he guides or participates in the audience's reactions, devices familiar to medieval storytellers, but rarely given the artistic coherence in a finished text independent of actual performance. In *Troilus and Criseyde* Chaucer has convincingly stylized in a permanent form the ephemeralness of a living entertainment and the mobility of actual delivery.

Yet the purpose of Chaucer as 'second author', if we may judge it from the development of the poem, as well as from its total effect, is surprisingly serious. He is handling a venerable story with dignity and with strong and deep moral and philosophical implications. His original audience we may assume was not expecting to take the performance quite so seriously as on reflection afterwards they would discover Chaucer had intended them to. The depth and range of the poem, announced with a disingenuous simplicity at the beginning, hinted at more confidently in the openings of the successive books, are only gradually disclosed in the narration and only fully revealed at the very end. Chaucer is not competing with his contemporaries, the 'makers' of vernacular romance:

> But litel book, no makyng thow n'envie,
> But subgit be to alle poesye;
> And kis the steppes, where as thow seest pace
> Virgile, Ovide, Omer, Lucan, and Stace.
>
> V 1789-92

And *poesye* is the title of honour Chaucer reserved for the work of the great poets of antiquity and Italy, whose achievements in this poem he emulates.

Thus as a composition the poem moves along two distinct lines. The *narratio* is visible enough. It is concerned with the story-material Chaucer took out of Boccaccio. It is with the telling of this story that the Narrator is kept busy. But there is in the poem a concern to describe a line of causality and destiny, which shall show the events of the story at a higher degree of generality. To recognize this line is not to abstract from the poem, not to disentangle a meaning or a message, for the line runs throughout the poem. The poet himself, not the Narrator, is in charge of this line. This is what the old rhetoricians called the *argumentum* of a piece of writing. Commentators on

Boethius' *Topics* called it the *vis sententiae*. It is the theme of a work in the actual process of evolving, the line of force along which the *narratio* is directed.

From the beginning of the poem we are conscious that the whole action is under the grip of a larger control. On the surface the Narrator presents it as 'the lawe of kynde' we are advised to follow. But the counterweight comes early, 'O blinde world, O blynde entencioun', a sombre murmur which gathers strength. The naive Narrator is another blind man leading blind men to their fates. We are acknowledging the *argumentum* when we realize the illusion implicit in the *narratio*. All the ways of the world, all the solemn dealings with sex and war which seem so compulsive and yet so uncontrollable, are neither one nor the other. As guides by themselves they work confusion, as values they are a vanity. The fixed and familiar courses down which men seek to outrun and outwit their fellows lead nowhere any man wishes to be. The world with its seemingly hard and inescapable conventions imaged in the poem is illusion, a necessary illusion, which exacts from us a disillusionment. Hope lies in another realm, scarcely related to the iron necessities of human society. The *argumentum* of the poem depends upon a melancholy, unsensationalized view of life, compounded out of a Christian quietism and a faintly sentimental stoicism. It reflects a mood of many Englishmen in the late fourteenth century.

In public Chaucer was no more than a minor functionary and his appearance in court would depend upon a reputation as a sophisticated entertainer, not as a speculative moralist or an interpreter of his times. The *narratio* must carry the *argumentum* very lightly. To the secret hearts and thoughts of men in high places he remained a stranger. What went on in public he could learn only by humble and deferential observation. He could earn a little licence for solemnity as well as for jest if he were sufficiently entertaining.

The poet's intention and the anticipated responses of this court audience control the strategy: which in brief was to introduce the story with a touch of disengaging flippancy, to develop it swiftly, brightly but elaborately, to let the passions and the responses of the audience run and gather head, and then to make his purpose plain when the emotional effects are irresistible. There is much jocularity and irony in the detail of the telling. But it is often mock-jocularity and the irony of enhancement. Chaucer talks a thing down in order to build it up.

The use of this sort of device indicates the delicacy of the whole task. Perhaps we can assume that a medieval audience, even the most sophisticated, was pretty inflammable. Most of the way the poet cannot go too far or too fast in evoking participation with the story and identification with its characters. The audience must not find its conventional values openly mocked by unrelieved catastrophe. So the

Narrator must maintain throughout something of that initial *naiveté*, lest he be held responsible for the calamity. The poet cannot make a moral too emphatically, so the Narrator cannot be seen to identify himself too steadily with the logic of the destinies involved, or pass too magisterial a judgment on the actors who suffer them. The poet has to satisfy a whole range of worldliness which appreciates display, luxury, leisure and the solid reassurance of wealth and power and rank. So the Narrator presents, quite simplemindedly, sequences of fashionable behaviour, moments of worldly triumph and success, counsels of conventional wisdom. Throughout the poem there is sufficient humour to placate the unsentimental, enough undiscussed absolutes to win the idealist, some unwounding cynicism to disarm the disillusioned. By using the Narrator the poet can recall the audience from an excessive engrossment in certain aspects of the story. The Narrator can be used to lighten the ominous, to anticipate and therefore blunt the distracting keenness of the miseries, and still, by exhibiting the degree of his own involvement, inject expectancy into a story of what is already foreseen.

In the practical management of his Narrator Chaucer had of course a duty towards himself. He had to write—probably this came easily enough to a writer of his experience—a part which would suit his own delivery, his own powers of expressiveness of voice, gesture and elocution. More important, the poet in putting the poem together had to maintain his own morale, to remain confident that what he was doing was worth doing, to refuse to lose his own way in the story, and to ensure that in working out his intention he should achieve what every author aims at in a major work, a continuing fall-out of meaning, which should sift slowly down into the memory and modify understanding. The *argumentum* must shine clear even though it may seem to annul in part the *narratio* that carries it forward.

Problems of narration at this degree of complexity and skill fascinated Chaucer. He was to devise new and more complicated problems for himself in the *Canterbury Tales*, which represent the ultimate achievement in medieval storytelling, when the mobile recession of the narrating voices is often as puzzling and ingenious as the construction of a Chinese box. Fortunately *Troilus and Criseyde* is easier to follow. It is all one story and its narrative advancing through the complexities of presentation is strong and clear.

From *Chaucer and Chaucerians: Critical Studies in Middle English Literature* (ed. D. S. Brewer), Nelson, 1966, pp. 71–75.

B. L. JEFFERSON

The Influence of the *Consolation* on *Troilus* and the *Knight's Tale*

... It has long been recognized that the *Consolation* has more influence on *Troilus* and the *Knight's Tale* than on any other of the longer poems of Chaucer. I have, therefore, found it advisable to consider these poems specially in relation to the *Consolation*. Such a study at once reveals that Chaucer did not use the Boethian material haphazardly for the interest that might be attached to particular lines in themselves, but that, as might be expected from the foregoing chapters, he brings its consideration of the fundamental questions of human existence to bear in a large way on the lives of his characters. Chaucer's thoughts must have been afire with the Boethian philosophy when he worked over these tales from their Italian originals, for always looming up in their background, as he worked them over, are the fundamental Boethian conceptions of fate and human felicity, determining his mental attitude toward the subject matter. *Troilus,* especially, offered Chaucer opportunity for a practical study in real life of the working out of the Boethian teaching. In the tale, as it was presented to him in the *Filostrato* of Boccaccio, he saw a capital example of the sudden reversal of Fortune's wheel, and an unusually interesting example of human falseness or lack of steadfastness, of worldly felicity, and of human affairs directed to a predetermined end by a relentless fate; and it will be found that most of the extended passages gathered by Chaucer from sources outside the immediate original, itself influenced somewhat by the *Consolation*, concern these very things. I shall now consider the two conceptions of fate and felicity as they are discussed in *Troilus* and in the *Knight's Tale*.

The fatalistic tendency in *Troilus* has often been commented upon, but Professor Kittredge, in his recent discussion of the poem,[1] for the first time reveals how important is an understanding of Chaucer's emphasis on fate for a full appreciation of the poem. Not only are the hero and heroine borne irresistibly to an inevitable doom, but their doom is linked inseparably with the larger doom of Troy; all are swept headlong to certain ruin. Chaucer heightens the effect by assuming an attitude of reluctance at being the narrator of events so tragic; but, having once begun, he must not draw back from his thankless task;

[1] *Chaucer and his Poetry*, pp. 108–145.

it is almost as if he too, by the mere act of narration, is drawn relentlessly into the course of destiny. The fate of Troilus and Criseyde
is the more terrible, because they themselves, aside from human frailties, do nothing to bring on the catastrophe. Even Criseyde commits no
overt act, but is led on from step to step by Pandarus, by circumstances,
and by her own spirit of curiosity, succumbing throughout to a tenderness of heart which she retains to the end and to her weakness in
character, her 'slydinge corage'. Her final unfaith, as a tragedy in
character, as her part in the 'double sorrow' which Chaucer is describing, I shall discuss more at length presently. Troilus and Criseyde,
thus, are the victims of a concatenation of circumstances largely outside of their own control. Pandarus, of course, attempts to manage
their affairs, but he is only a link in the chain of fate, a 'fly on the
chariot wheel'. Nothing may stem the tide on which they are driven
by 'necessitee'.

The machinery by which fate operates in *Troilus* is entirely
Boethian. It is true that the gods must be the gods of classical mythology as the tale concerns ancient Troy, but the attributes which they
possess are the attributes of the Boethian deity, and what is said
about them to a great extent will be found in the *Consolation*. Almost
every phase of the Boethian discussion of Providence is represented.
His scheme of the hierarchy of providential agencies is recognized.
Jove, of his wise 'purveyaunce', grants to the Parcae or Fates, and
to the goddess Fortune the execution of the destinal ordinances, just
as described in the *Consolation*. Fortune is given a very high rank
among the gods, and is honoured by Troilus above all the others.
Chance is regarded by the characters as of great significance. Events
happen by 'necessitee'. There are also brought up in *Troilus* the two
questions which lead respectively to the discussions of the fourth and
fifth books of the *Consolation:* namely, how may a just god permit evil
and how is free will in man possible in the face of so unescapable a
destinal control. The most remarkable departure from classical
mythology, perhaps, is in the case of the god of love. This god in
Troilus, not at all the mischievous young archer of conventional
love poetry, is given all the qualities of the celestial love described
so at length by Boethius; and to the description of the might of
this god throughout all the universe Chaucer devotes almost one
hundred lines. The 'bond of love' in the *Consolation* is a poetic
conception, and, accordingly, belongs mainly to the *meters* and not to
the more matter of fact *proses* where pure reason rather than poetic
inspiration is the guide. Chaucer apparently recognized this distinction; accordingly, in a poem like *Troilus* he may express himself in
terms of the 'bond of love', a liberty which he does not take in a more
genuinely philosophical poem like *Truth* or *Lack of Stedfastness*.
And throughout *Troilus* it is necessary to remember that he is using the

Boethian material poetically and artistically and that, as a complete master of it, he is adapting it to the purposes of the poem . . . .

In the *Knight's Tale,* which is less a psychological study than *Troilus,* there is less contrast between the characters; but even here there is evidence of a careful selection of the Boethian material. It is commonly known that the *Knight's Tale* is full of the influence of the *Consolation,* but it may not be realized that the greater part of this influence is concentrated into three long speeches, one allotted to Arcite, one to Palamon, and one to Theseus; that each one of these speeches is on a common theme; and that this theme is the relation of Providence to man's happiness, a point which it is the prime object of the *Consolation* to discuss, and a point which Chaucer made much of in *Troilus,* as we have just seen. Arcite, ill satisfied with events, wonders why he cannot understand the wise purveyance of God, who does all things for the best; but he blames himself for stumbling around so blindly for false happiness—such stumbling as Dame Philosophy describes in 3. p2. Palamon, on the other hand, does not blame himself, but takes the benighted position in which Boethius describes himself at the outset of the *Consolation*; he, like Boethius in I. m5, cries out against the cruel gods who permit innocent men to suffer. Theseus blames neither God nor himself, but, by explaining the origin of the universe and the divine plan, shows, as Dame Philosophy does in 4. p6, m6, that there is an established order to which men must submit and which turns all things to good; his speech might be summed up in Chaucer's line, 'trouthe shal delivere, hit is no drede', as explained elsewhere (pp. 116ff. above). That the distinctions between the three speeches were not calculated by Chaucer, it is difficult to believe. Palamon's speech follows immediately after that of Arcite, and the proximity of the two intensifies the contrast between them. Impressions of the characters are given which extend throughout the poem. More pity is aroused for Arcite, and he who acknowledges that God's ways are always just meets in the moment of his greatest triumph a sudden and tragic death, whereas Palamon who complains against heaven receives the high reward. The speech of Theseus, to be sure, softens down the tragic end of Arcite, but at the same time it points back to the speeches of the two younger and less wise men and is made to appear more noble and dignified by a contrast with theirs. . . .

The thesis shows that Chaucer worked over the *Consolation of Philosophy,* in his translation of that work, earnestly, making use of the Latin original and a French translation, not to mention the commentary of Trivet and his possible recourse to various texts of the original; that he attempted, although not always quite succeeding, to reproduce the thought of the *Consolation* faithfully and to reproduce its spirit by a stateliness of tone and by embellishments of style; that he subsequently incorporated in extended passages here and there throughout his poetry and individual poems almost all of the *Consolation*— what it has to say of fortune, of false felicity, power, fame, and riches, of true gentility, of the two 'points' of blissfulness, fortitude of spirit and truth, of fate, and of the connected subjects, the relation of evil and free will to a benevolent and all-powerful deity, although he seems to have emphasized fate at the expense of the latter two; that his grasp of the *Consolation* was so firm that he was able beautifully to express its central teachings in the short poem *Truth* as counsel to Sir Philip la Vache and to put it to uses so original that its influence, although possibly profound, is transmuted almost beyond recognition as in the *House of Fame*; that the *Consolation*, as it concerns the most important question of life, the end or 'fyn' of existence, went far to determine his mental attitude, his conception and disposition of the characters in the *Knight's Tale* and especially in *Troilus*, two poems presumably written when he was fresh from the translation; that the *Consolation* was a lasting, if a diminishing influence, throughout the *Canterbury Tales*, especially in the discussions of gentilesse.

How much the *Consolation* determined Chaucer's own attitude toward life, it is difficult to determine with precision. At the least, it may be said that Boethius and Chaucer were compatible in point of view and that Chaucer found in Boethius, in many ways, a congenial spirit. At the most, it may be said that Boethius was an influence so profound that he completely determined Chaucer's view of the meaning of life and of the way in which life should be conducted. The truth no doubt lies somewhere between the two extremes, and Boethius probably accentuated and extended views which Chaucer already had temperamentally. Furthermore, the *Consolation of Philosophy*, as it thus gives expression to a philosophy of life which so much interested Chaucer, presents an opportunity to determine what Chaucer's conception of the ideal philosopher would be. Chaucer's ideal philosopher would be a man who understood and brought into practice the two 'points' of the *Consolation*. First, as the aged Egeus, father of Theseus, he must understand the transmutation of the world from woe to weal and back to woe again, and, unheeding worldly joys and woes alike, must stand steadfast, at peace with himself, though the world fall in ruin about him. But he must do more than stand stoically and grimly at bay. He must realize, somewhat like Plato, that there is an ideal good and that this good is unalterable; that, through a study of astronomy, so as to understand the harmony of divine law and to obtain a just perspective of petty worldly concerns, and through gentilesse and through the truth within him, he must try to associate himself with the universal good. When one remembers Chaucer's *Astrolabe, Melibeus*, and *Parson's Tale*, his retirement from life poring over old books, his broad and sympathetic view of his fellow men of all degrees and conditions, it is almost possible to believe that Chaucer himself was this kind of philosopher, although, as he himself says, 'no man is al trewe, I gesse'. The above pages help to show that Chaucer was sometimes a very serious poet and that he, not always earth-bound, had visions of eternal truths such as the greatest poets have had.

From *Chaucer and the* 'Consolation of Philosophy of Boethius', Princeton University Press, 1917, pp. 120–22, 130–31, 165–66. Four footnotes have been omitted.

The Good Wife of Juxta Bathon

. . . Alisoun is not, strictly speaking, 'of Bathe', but 'of biside Bathe'. Chaucer may have meant his fourteenth-century audience to identify the Wife by this detail; but for us, the localization of the Wife's parish only serves to make her seem more actual than she would otherwise be. Manly points out that Bath in Chaucer's time was 'still confined almost entirely within its ancient walls and lay in a loop of the river Avon, which surrounded it on the east and south and about half the west side.' Outside the north gate, Manly continues, there had sprung up 'the parish of St Michael-without-the-Walls, or St Michael-without-the-North-Gate—also sometimes designated as *juxta Bathon*'. This little parish was formed by two short streets meeting at an acute angle which had the vertex at the north gate; facing the gate was 'the ancient square-towered church of St. Michael', the very church, so Manly suggests, at the door of which each of Alisoun's numerous matrimonial adventures began.[1]

The Wife, as befits her station in life, has an occupation in which she is highly skilled:

> Of clooth-makyng she hadde swich an haunt
> She passed hem of Ypres and of Gaunt.
>
> (ll. 447–448)

St Michael-juxta-Bathon was indeed a parish largely devoted to weaving—and 'wherever the cloth industry flourished in England, women were prominent in it'.[2] But the praise heaped upon the Wife's expertness (after all, to surpass the weavers of 'Ypres' and of 'Gaunt' would be to do better than the best) is Chaucer's way of saying that that is what Alisoun herself thinks of her own weaving; perhaps there is an ironical twist, also, in the words, for the West country weavers, far from being the best, did not enjoy too good a reputation.[3] One is ready to take the Wife at her own valuation, however; the force of her personality pushes through the written words, and demands that one believe.

> In al the parisshe wif ne was ther noon
> That to the offrynge bifore hire sholde goon;

[1] Manly, *New Light*, pp. 231 f.
[2] Manly, *Cant. Tales*, p. 527, n. 445.
[3] Manly quotes from Atton and Holland (*The King's Customs*, p. 26) in support of this statement.

G

> And if ther dide, certeyn so wrooth was she,
> That she was out of alle charitee.

(ll. 449–452)

Of course, Dame Alisoun feels that she must be first wherever precedence is held to be valuable! And the order of precedence in making the offering was a matter of concern in the Middle Ages. Chaucer's Parson, for example, in speaking of the 'harmes that cometh of Pride' mentions the kind of Pride which 'waiteth first to be salewed er he wole salewe, . . . and eek he waiteth or desireth to sitte, or elles to goon above hym in the wey, . . . or goon to offryng biforn his neighebor';[4] Deschamps, too, refers more than once to this custom of allowing importance in the community to determine the order in which the congregation went up to make their offerings in church.[5] But the fact that Dame Alisoun is so wrathful that she is 'out of alle charitee' when someone usurps what she considers to be her rightful place is an indication, not of conceit, but of frank pride in achievement. Alisoun is never troubled by false modesty!

We expect a successful and friendly woman of affairs to care about her appearance and the impression she makes on others. The Wife of Bath does not disappoint us in this respect.

> Hir coverchiefs ful fyne weren of ground;
> I dorste swere they weyeden ten pound
> That on a Sonday weren upon hir heed.
> Hir hosen weren of fyn scarlet reed,
> Ful streite yteyd, and shoes ful moyste and newe.
> Boold was hir face, and fair, and reed of hewe.
>
> Upon an amblere esily she sat,
> Ywympled wel, and on hir heed an hat
> As brood as is a bokeler or a targe;
> A foot-mantel aboute hir hipes large,
> And on hir feet a paire of spores sharpe.

(ll. 453–458, 469–473)

It is true that Dame Alisoun is conspicuously overdressed on Sundays, but is not this by design? Why should she not let the world see that she is successful enough to warrant fine clothes of good material? Her wearing of such garments stamps her as the most prosperous woman of business in St Michael-juxta-Bathon, and naturally she takes pleasure 'to se, and eek for to be seye' as she later tells us with gusto in her own *Prologue,* and adds that much usage keeps the moths from *her* beautiful scarlet apparel.[6] We need not believe, then, that Chaucer

---

[4] X (I) 407.
[5] In *Le Miroir de Mariage,* ll. 3289–3290, Deschamps writes—
. . . va la plus grande
Devant les aultres a l'offrande.
See also ll. 3316–3323, 3376–3378.
[6] III (D) 552 ff.

is exaggerating when he writes of Alisoun's ten-pound 'coverchiefs' which were so finely textured ('ful fyne of ground'). The *coverchief* of the Middle Ages was a veil-like structure which was arranged in folds over the head;[7] the coverchief could be simple and light, or elaborate and heavy. The Wife's scarlet hose, also part of her festival attire, are always tightly and neatly drawn ('ful streite yteyd'), and the shoes which complete this imposing costume are of new and supple ('moyste') leather.

The Wife's dress for the pilgrimage, however, is much more sensible. True, her hat is as broad as a shield ('a bokeler or a targe'),[8] but it is firmly placed on her trimly wimpled head; and she is careful enough to wear a protective outer skirt (a 'foot-mantel')[9] about her ample hips, when she rides her 'amblere'. An ambling horse (often called a pacer today) is one which has been taught to lift two feet together on the same side of its body, making for comfortable riding on a long journey, and is therefore precisely the mount an experienced traveller such as Alisoun would choose. And since Alisoun wears a 'paire' of sharp spurs, we know she rides astride, as most women of her class did in Chaucer's time.[10]

The Wife of Bath's orderly and well set-up appearance, as has been suggested, is in keeping with the strong directness of her character. She is one who has always known exactly what she wants and exactly how to get it. She desires, and has obtained importance in her community; good times with gay companions—

> In felaweshipe wel koude she laughe and carpe;
> (l. 474)

a wide variety of love affairs; and, as we shall hear, the excitements and pleasures of travel. The Wife of Bath leads a systematized life for all its florid quality, and so her bold countenance, 'reed of hewe', escapes being blowzy and is attractive in its vigour.

Throughout the years, Dame Alisoun has been, perhaps, most famous—or infamous—for her marital and extra-marital adventures:

> She was a worthy womman al hire lyve:
> Housbondes at chirche dore she hadde fyve,

---

[7] Druitt, pp. 239–244, 246, 264. The monumental brasses of Chaucer's time which show 'ladies of quality' wearing the coverchief do not support Manly's statement (*New Light*, pp. 230 f.) that this head-covering had not been 'in style' since the middle of the century.

[8] A 'bokeler' was synonymous with 'targe' (*NED*); the Yeoman, it will be remembered, carries a bokeler, or small round shield, used to ward off blows.

[9] *NED*, 'Foot-mantel'.

[10] Manly says (*Cant. Tales*, p. 528, n. 473) that Queen Anne, wife of Richard II, introduced the side-saddle for women, and Robinson (p. 765) also makes this statement. Manly calls attention to an early fifteenth-century illumination (plate opp. p. 192 of his *Cant. Tales*) in which ladies of the court ride side-saddle. In the Ellesmere MS, in which the Wife of Bath is depicted as riding astride, the Prioress is depicted as riding side-saddle.

Withouten oother compaignye in youthe,—
But therof nedith nat to speke as nowthe.

(ll. 459–462)

Chaucer's contemporaries could not have been as startled as we are
by the number of Alisoun's husbands, for, as Dr Coulton writes, 'the
extreme promptitude with which the Wife of Bath provided herself
with a new husband . . . is characteristically medieval.'[11] A woman
of any property in the Middle Ages found it as difficult to remain
single as the dowerless daughter to marry: no matter how unwilling
the woman with even a few possessions might be to enter into a
marriage contract, which as a rule was literally just that, a cut-and-
dried bargain, some man with a covetous eye upon her worldly goods
would compel her, using violent means if necessary, to marry him. If
the lady were willing, as Alisoun too plainly always was, it would
be unthinkable that she should remain a widow no matter how frequently she might temporarily arrive at that state. Chaucer's audience,
therefore, would not have found the fact of the Wife's five husbands
astonishing or intrinsically humorous, but they undoubtedly looked
forward with a keen relish to hearing the details of Alisoun's management of her various consorts; an Alisoun in any period of history is
so obviously born 'to han the governaunce' in wedded life!

But the Alisouns of the medieval world were certainly in the
minority; the lot of most women in Chaucer's time was not one of
mastery or of freedom. The common sentiment that 'woman is man's
ruin,' was backed by the firm conviction that all females were created
as vastly inferior to males.[12] A woman should never strive with her
husband, writes the Knight of la Tour Landry, and proceeds to tell
the story of the justifiable fate of a wife who dared to place herself on an
equal footing with her husband. The latter was so angered by his wife's
attempts at 'governaunce' that he knocked her down, thus breaking
her nose so that her face was permanently 'foule blemisshed'. Hence,
concludes the Knight of la Tour Landry, one sees that a wife ought
silently to permit her husband to be the master, 'for that is her wor-
shippe'.[13] We are reminded by this edifying 'ensaumple' that the
Wife of Bath has suffered a physical injury for a like cause—

But she was somdel deef, and that was scathe.

(l. 446)

We find out later that, after considerable provocation, Alisoun's fifth
husband, the 'som tyme clerk of Oxenford', in a vain effort to assert
his male superiority once struck the intractable Alisoun about the ears
so violently that her hearing is now impaired.[14]

[11] Coulton, *Ch. and his Eng.*, p. 204.
[12] *Ibid.*, Chap. XVI *passim*.
[13] La Tour Landry, p. 25.
[14] III (D) 666 ff.

Dr Owst suggests that the ultimate source of the Wife of Bath is the woman in the Book of Proverbs[15] who is 'subtil of heart'. Fourteenth-century preachers turn again and again to this passage, expanding the interpretation to meet the exigencies of a particular sermon or the homilist's fancy. Too many modern women are 'foolish', the sermons say: these women lay snares to entrap men instead of chastely staying at home with their husbands, they talk too much and love gossip, they deck themselves in unseemly finery.[16] One preacher, for example, speaks of 'a foolish woman, garrulous and vagrant, impatient of quiet, not able to keep her feet within the house, now she is without, now in the streets', never constant.[17] And worst of all are the women who will not submissively follow out the wishes of their husbands.[18] But whether Dame Alisoun owes her existence in part to sermon-complaints, or whether the sermon-complaints were brought about because there were enough actual women like Alisoun to warrant the pulpit dissatisfaction, cannot be determined. As Dr Coulton points out, 'In every generation moralists noted with pain the gradual emancipation of ladies from a restraint which had always been excessive, and had often been merely theoretical.'[19] Perhaps Chaucer, in creating Alisoun, drew on both homily and the actual New Woman of his day; whatever the case, his audience must have greeted Alisoun as irresistibly amusing and lifelike.

Chaucer speaks of the five husbands whom Alisoun has had 'at chirche dore', a reference to a custom which has no modern counterpart. According to George Elliott Howard, the medieval York ritual, still extant, is typical of any medieval marriage service; it directs that 'the ceremony takes place before the church door, . . . the man standing "on the right of the woman and the woman on the left of the man" '.[20] The priest's duty is then to ask the banns in the mother-tongue, after which the ceremony proceeds in striking similarity to that used now in the English Church. As Howard states, the use of the vernacular is important as it indicates that the bride and groom were regarded as the real actors in the ceremony, and the priest as merely leader and teacher; perhaps this lay nature of the ceremony entirely explains why it was not performed within the church. The vernacular was probably used also so that the witnesses would understand what was being done. After the couple were married, they and the witnesses

[15] Proverbs, VII, 10–12.
[16] Owst, *Lit. and Pulpit*, pp. 385–404 *passim*.
[17] *Ibid.*, p. 385 f. (Quotation from MS Add. 21253, fol. 45 b.)
[18] *Ibid.*, p. 389. Dr Owst writes (n. 2) that no part of the *Canterbury Tales* 'illustrates better the debt of contemporary thought and literature to the pulpit' than does the *Wife of Bath's Prologue*.
And, as has been pointed out in this chapter, the Wife of Bath's portrait in the *General Prologue* is a summary of her own *Prologue*.
[19] Coulton, *Ch. and his Eng.*, p. 220.
[20] Howard, *Hist. Mat. Inst.*, I, 303.

entered the church, and the priest officiated at the nuptial mass, which
was, of course, sung in Latin.[21]

Aside from Dame Alisoun's fifth marriage (which she herself
engineered), Alisoun's amorous adventures have had little to do with
wedded bliss. In her own *Prologue* the Wife dilates upon those
experiences in love she has had with 'compaignye' other than dull
husbands; in the *General Prologue* we note that Chaucer passes over
these experiences with humorous discretion, although he subtly
epitomizes and emphasizes them a few lines later by saying—

> Of remedies of love she knew per chaunce,
> For she koude of that art the olde daunce.
>
> (ll. 475–476)

The 'remedies of love', which Alisoun knows so well, is an allusion
to Ovid's *Remedia Amoris,* a work familiar to some at least of
Chaucer's audience.[22] The jest lies, of course, in Alisoun's knowledge of the *Remedia,* rather than the *Ars Amatoria:* she knows all
the rules of the game, is a figure used by Chaucer more than once.[23]

Of the Wife of Bath's interests, second in importance only to her
love affairs is her fondness for travelling in gay company:

> And thries hadde she been at Jerusalem;
> She hadde passed many a straunge strem;
> At Rome she hadde been, and at Boloigne,
> In Galice at Seint Jame, and at Cologne.
> She koude muchel of wandrynge by the weye.
> Gat-tothed was she, soothly for to seye.
>
> (ll. 463–468)

That Chaucer couples the fact that the Wife has her teeth set wide
apart with her fondness for crossing 'many a straunge strem' would
seem to substantiate Skeat's statement that the Middle Ages interpreted
this physical characteristic as a sign of much travel and of good fortune.[24] Chaucer's later allusion to the same characteristic of the

---

[21] *Ibid.,* 303–310. Coulton suggests (*Med. Pan.,* p. 397) that since evidence
in the Middle Ages was often hard to procure, 'general notoriety was of
extreme value' and marriage at the church door was performed to make the
ceremony as public as possible and thus obtain the maximum number of
witnesses. Witnesses were extremely important in marriage services.

[22] Haskins writes (*Renaissance of Twelfth Cent.,* pp. 107 ff.) that the
medieval vogue of Ovid was continuous down to Chaucer and later writers.
All of Ovid's works were read, especially the *Metamorphoses,* the *Art of Love,*
and the *Remedies of Love.*

[23] See VI (C) 79 and *Troilus and Criseyde,* III, 695. The expression was
also common in the French of the time (see Langlois's note on l. 3936 of the
Rom. de la Rose—'Qu'el set toute la vielle dance').

[24] Skeat, V, 44, n. 468. I have not been able to find evidence supporting
Skeat's statement that the gap-toothed person was thought to be lucky, other
than the anonymous note he himself cites, a note appearing in the 'Folk Lore'
section of *Notes and Queries,* First Series, VI (1852), 601, which merely
states that teeth set wide apart are a sign of luck. On the other hand, the

Wife's,[25] however, supports Professor Curry's contention that the fourteenth-century audience might think of a gap-toothed person as 'envious, irreverent, luxurious by nature, bold, deceitful, faithless, and suspicious'.[26] Professor Barnouw some years ago pointed out that women who were 'gap-toothed by nature' were thought in the Middle Ages 'to be predestined for the office of love'.[27] But are we not justified in supposing that all three 'signs' were in the minds of Chaucer's contemporaries? Certainly Alisoun's flamboyant personality bears them all out.

We should expect the Wife of Bath to be particularly eager, then, to go on pilgrimages for two reasons; the pilgrimage was the most popular form of travel for pleasure, indeed practically the only kind of such travel, and especially appealed to women who would escape from the restrictions imposed by a husband.[28] It would be like Dame Alisoun to select the most important and the liveliest of the customary pilgrimages.

Besides the Holy Land, four places in the Middle Ages were 'noted as being centres of greater pilgrimage': Rome, Compostella ('in Galice'), Canterbury, and Cologne.[29] When we meet the Wife of Bath, she is on her way to Canterbury, and she has already made the other important pilgrimages. She has been three times to Jerusalem, as well as to the less important 'Boloigne'. Chaucer is not exaggerating when he writes that the Wife knows a good deal about 'wandrynge by the weye'. . . .

The question as to whether or not Chaucer drew on Jean de Meun's La Vieille in the Roman de la Rose for the portait of the Wife of Bath is not of great importance to us who are meeting the Wife principally in the General Prologue. In the Wife's own Prologue, a great many of the phrases assigned to La Vieille are borrowed by the English poet for his Alisoun's use,[30] but in the General Prologue only one parallel to what La Vieille says is found: the Wife of Bath has had 'oother compaignye in youthe'—La Vieille boasts that she ignored a number of would-be lovers when she was young, for 'j'avoie autre compaignie'.[31] Furthermore, as Mead so convincingly

belief that such teeth presage travel for those possessing them survives as a superstition even today in Kentucky (*Kentucky Superstitions*, 865), which is proof that at least seventeenth-century England was accepting this physical characteristic to be a sign of travel; and as folk-superstition seldom springs up overnight, it seems probable that a superstition accepted in 1600 might well have its roots in 1400.

[25] III (D) 603.
[26] Curry, *Ch. and Med. Sci.*, p. 109.
[27] Barnouw, *The Nation*, CIII, 540.
[28] III (D) 655–58, 550–59.
[29] *Cath. Ency.*, 'Pilgrimage'.
[30] Fansler (*Ch. and R. R.*, pp. 168 f.) lists thirty-five parallels between the *Wife of Bath's Prologue* and the *Rom. de la Rose*.
[31] *Rom. de la Rose*, l. 12781.

points out, the essential character of La Vieille is fundamentally different from that of Alisoun. La Vieille is old, decrepit, through with life; the Wife of Bath has still many years to live, she is vigorous and imbued with *joie de vivre*. La Vieille is morose; the Wife is good-natured, even when she is occasionally shrewish.[32] Chaucer may have taken words from the French poem, but Dame Alisoun is straight from life.

As a matter of interest, we must not take leave of the Wife of Bath before we have examined briefly the detailed 'horoscope' Professor Curry has so learnedly cast for her.[33] Using the data which the Wife gives in her *Prologue* (she was born at a time when Venus and Mars were in conjunction in Taurus)[34] and quoting from the medieval authorities on 'astronomye', Professor Curry shows that Alisoun is the victim of her stars: Venus by herself would make Alisoun beautiful and graceful, and would provide Alisoun with a delicate complexion, but Mars distorts the figure into heaviness ('hir hipes large' come from this planet's 'excessive virility'), and makes the face 'reed of hewe'. The Wife's voice, which through Venus alone would be sweet and well-modulated, is because of Mars, 'raised continually in vulgar jest and indelicate banter'.[35]

> For certes, I am al Venerien
> In feelynge, and myn herte is Marcien,[36]

confesses Alisoun, meaning, as Professor Curry indicates, that she would like to be charming, joyous, and pleasure-loving in the most refined sense, as well as appealing to the opposite sex in a highly ladylike fashion, but that Mars has debased these characteristics into rowdiness, boisterous spirits, a fondness for questionable 'wandrynge by the weye', and the unrestrained attractiveness of the 'healthy and frank female animal'.[37] But again, as Professor Curry says, it is unlikely that Chaucer drew the portrait of the vivid personality of the Wife of Bath from anything but life.[38] Hence the horoscope is merely an addition to the picture, and its introduction in the Wife's *Prologue* furnishes us with another of Chaucer's witty and realistic touches.

From *A Commentary on the General Prologue to the* 'Canterbury Tales', Macmillan, New York, 1948, pp. 214–226.

[32] Mead, *PMLA*, XVI, 394 f.
[33] Curry, *op. cit.*, pp. 91–118.
[34] III (D) 600 ff.
[35] Curry, *op. cit.*, pp. 108 f.
[36] III (D) 609–610.
[37] Curry, *op. cit.*, pp. 109 ff.
[38] *Ibid.*, p. 117.   Manly calls our attention (*New Light*, pp. 232 ff.) to Chaucer's probable visits to the royal forest of Petherton when he acted as one of the deputy foresters; to make such visits Chaucer would have ridden through St Michael-juxta-Bathon. Manly adds that 'Alysoun' seems to be the commonest name for women in the *Ancient Deeds* of Bath—and more than one of these Alices 'rejoiced in three or more husbands'!

RUTH NEVO

Motive and Mask in the
General Prologue

... As we read the *Prologue* we become aware of a certain family
resemblance between the pilgrims, despite their diversity. Or rather,
as character is subtly, almost imperceptibly revealed, we become aware
of a persistent criterion of selection operating upon the data provided
by observation. It is not, of course, that every objective detail given in
the description is chosen according to this single principle. What we
do find is that there is no portrait, however short, without its reference,
direct or indirect, to the matter of money. The pilgrim's characteristic behaviour is defined in every case in terms of the acquisition and
use of wealth. The 'goodness' of the good characters, and the 'bad-
ness' of the bad or questionable characters are both exhibited with
reference to this criterion, and in the characters towards whom there is
an ironic attitude the irony inheres in the evident discrepancy between
profession and action with regard to this same matter. Since there is
little, save sex, in social life more productive of diverse possibility on
the one hand, nor on the other more readily susceptible to overriding
moral judgment, than the individual's attitude to his worldly goods, or
his status in terms of worldly goods, such an analysis has the double
advantage of a fixed point and a spectrum. Money—pelf—is the touch-
stone to which each of these characters is brought, and by which he is
tested. There is no portrait which does not take its orientation from
an attitude to money or from dealings with money, whether in the form
of illicit gain or of legitimate hire.

It is not only the Doctor, who loved gold in special because gold in
physic is a cordial; in the house of the hospitable Franklin it snows
meat and drink; and the Merchant's success, it is slyly and acutely
implied, is due to his skill in not letting anyone know when he is in
debt, while his interest in the 'keeping of the Sea' between Middle-
burgh and Orewelle is patently not purely patriotic. Furthermore,
whether he is a Merchant Adventurer, or a Stapler exporting wool,
illicit currency deals are apparently a mainstay of his business. The
Shipman can be trusted in charge of craft in difficult seas and has
moreover sufficiently his wits about him to draw a draught of wine
while the Chapman sleeps; the 'sclendre cholerich' Reeve knows well
enough how to feather his own nest, while attending to his master's

affairs, as his own 'faire wonying' shows; and his colleague, the Manciple, knows better than any of the students of the Middle Temple how to make a spendthrift nobleman's budget balance. The Friar's *In Principio* is so effective that it is able to extract the last farthing from a poor widow; the Prioress's penchant for high life extends to the choice and costly fare—roasted flesh, milk and wastel bread—on which her 'smale houndes' are fed; the Monk quite blatantly spares no expense either upon his table or his stable. The wives of the Guildsmen, those fair burgesses, are not averse to being called Madame and leading the procession to vigils, privileges they enjoy by virtue of their husbands' 'catel and rente'; and these respectable aldermen, together with the Cook, worthy, to judge from the delicacies he provides, of his temporary hire, are contrasted with the rumbustious Miller, the stout Carl who is master of the art of stealing corn and taking triple toll for grinding. The Lawyer, besides being well provided with fees, and robes, by his clients, is a great purchaser of land, of which he invariably succeeds in getting unrestricted possession. That precious pair, the Summoner and the Pardoner, will be treated separately; here it is perhaps enough to point out the Summoner's way with the archdeacon's curse (ll. 653 ff.), and the quite unironical flat statement in the Pardoner's portrait,

> But with thise relikes, whan that he had fond
> A povre person dwellynge up-on lond,
> Up-on a day he gat him moore moneye
> Than that the person gat in monthes tweye.
> And thus, with feyned flaterye and japes,
> He made the person and the peple his apes.   (l. 701–706)

The Parson, to turn to the credit side of the human balance-sheet, is 'a good shepherd and no mercenarie'; the Plowman a good worker, living in peace and charity, working often without hire to help others, paying his own tithes faithfully; the Student's single coat is threadbare because he is too unworldly to get him a benefice; the Knight's coat, on the other hand, is still stained by the armour of his service in the cause of God. His son, to be sure, is a fashionable young man, but his courtesy is of the kind which by long-accepted definition is untouched by shadow of lucre, as is the yeoman service of the sturdy green-clad forester who is his retainer.

All these people have, of course, other and various attributes: they are sly, lecherous, quarrelsome, bawdy, vain, cheerful; and the stars in their courses have had much to do with their dispositions and predispositions.[1] But their *motivation* springs from a single source— Mammon; and it is this which provides the dynamic of the *Prologue* to the *Canterbury Tales* and the master key to its design. . . .

It has often been remarked that Chaucer chose, as with a stroke

[1] As W. C. Curry has shown in *Chaucer and the Medieval Sciences*, Oxford, 1926, revised edition, Allen and Unwin, 1960.

of genius, the only two places in England where this multifarious throng would all be likely to meet on equal terms—an Inn and a Cathedral; and the circumstance—a pilgrimage—which could credibly unite them in a common purpose.

Yet the idea of the pilgrimage is even more important to the conception and design of the *Canterbury Tales* than such a comment gives reason to think. On the supposition that Chaucer wished merely to paint a national portrait gallery and accordingly 'chose to measure the world by its smiling self rather than by the Kingdom of Heaven',[2] the pilgrimage has indeed no more than an accidental value in providing a common meeting-place and a common journey. It can be argued, however, that it is, on the contrary, quintessential, being the structural frame within which the Chaucerian irony operates, and a chief means whereby Chaucer reveals that it was in fact by the Kingdom of Heaven that he was measuring his world.

For that which, as we have seen, serves as a constant principle of selection in the descriptive portraits, serves also as a constant criterion of moral judgment operative throughout the *General Prologue.* Every character passes, or does not pass, the test of worldliness. The cavalcade unrolls before our eyes, detail after detail falls subtly, unerringly into place and we become aware of a universal category. They are worldlings, worldlings all. Save for the defender of the faith, the good pastor, the honest plowman, and the patient, unworldly scholar, these Canterbury pilgrims in festive journey to a Christian martyr's shrine, are totally taken up with the world and the flesh. They are worldlings in the fullest sense of the word—adjusted to the world, committed to the world, worldly wise. The world is their natural element. But it is within the framework of the pilgrimage that the dimension of irony is added to the meticulous descriptions. Not a word is lost, not an item wasted in the presence of the uncompromising fact represented by Canterbury.

The irony, so elusive as to have eluded many an honest critic, has been found special enough to merit the defining adjective 'Chaucerian'. Its mechanism is deceptively simple, its force the result of absolute consistency. Locally, in each portrait, it is the views and standards and criteria of the world that are assumed. The Prioress's fine manners, the Monk's fat swans and 'deynte' horses, the Merchant's 'chevysaunce', the Wife of Bath's magnificent kerchiefs, the Summoner's good fellowship—these in the eyes of the world are no great matter, are even desirable values. But at certain significant points—the Wife of Bath so wroth that she was out of all charity if preceded in the procession to offering; or *Amor vincit omnia*; or the Kingdom of Mammon again and again in an unremitting iteration; or the presence of the virtuous, the pure in spirit, the unmercenary—these views, standards and

[2] Coghill, *The Poet Chaucer*, Oxford, 1949, p. 124.

criteria are set by implication in absolute opposition to another absolute demand:

> The hye God, on whom that we bileeve
> In wilful poverte chees to lyve his lyf.

Chaucer is tolerant of his worldlings, profoundly so, but with a tolerance which is not moral leniency. It does not spring from a desire to excuse or mitigate their worldliness: there is no question, for instance, of his exonerating the Monk's travesty of the cloister in the name of gracious living.[3] Such venial 'tolerance' is no part of Chaucer's moral sensibility. Nor is it indeed part of the moral sensibility of an age which witnessed the Lollard risings, and more than once records its own version of puritan strictness of conscience. His tolerance has deeper roots—in a profound and equable conviction of human frailty. Irony, not invective, is his medium; and it implies no compromise. And the famous geniality springs not from whatever may be understood by such much used phrases as 'warm humanity' or 'love of life' but from the serenity of a perfect sense of moral proportion, and from joy in the exercise of a crystal-clear intelligence and a mastered literary art.

The intensity of the irony in the portraits is a function of the degree of discrepancy between profession and action in each of the characters portrayed. Chaucer evidently expects less from a Miller or a Man of Law than from a Prioress, a Monk or a Pardoner. Nevertheless the two possibilities, of virtue and of corruption, are constantly entertained of cleric and layman alike; and it is in this connection that the continuity of the Mammon theme performs its remarkable double service. It links the universe of socio-economic actualities to the universe of moral values. For while corruption shows itself in the abuse or exploitation of a socio-economic function this is the local and particular expression of a more general evil, which is operative in the structure of private personality before it manifests itself in the performance of public office. It was defined by Shelley as 'the principle of self of which money is the visible incarnation'. Cupidity is its best name, a conception more inclusive than greed or avarice, and one which can easily and justly be conveyed by the images of getting and spending, images through which it is focused though not exhausted.[4]

---

[3] The claim has been seriously made, for example, that 'his style of living, irreligious though it be, has a certain dignity about it . . . custom has lent a kind of warrant to the misuse of the funds . . . their inheritance brings with it something more than mere wealth: a measure of sophistication and cultivation which enables them to live graciously, as well as pleasantly' (Malone, op. cit. p. 176). Austin may indeed have his swynk to hiim reserved!

[4] A. W. Hoffmann, 'Chaucer's Prologue to Pilgrimage: The Two Voices' (E.H.L. XXI (1954)) has an analysis of the Prologue's other images of 'cupidity'. He finds the two voices of love—natural and divine, profane and redemptive,

The Wife of Bath may stand as the garrulous spokesman for all the weaker brethren among her fellow-travellers. She has her own rights in the long debate on the virtue of women which links several of the tales. But no one would claim that her version of married bliss exemplifies the principle of self transcended. When, on the other hand, she argues that virginity is great perfection—for those who wish to be perfect—she exemplifies the easy-going conscience of the majority of the pilgrims. Once the self permits its own exclusion from the moral order it itself acknowledges, the essential breach is made, and the way is open for every kind of cupidity and every kind of rationalization. The way of this world is a practical application of Lear's thundered forbearance, 'None does offend, none I say, none'. But Lear was mad. His mind had broken down under the stress of unaccustomed insight. These pious pilgrims are as sane as can be, and no doctrine could better suit their lax, self-palliating souls. They have all excluded themselves from the rules. Self-indulgent cupidity is the law of their being, and the pursuit of pelf, with all that goes along with it, its chief and most prominent manifestation in the context of social relations. On this view, of course, Chaucer's apology for his neglect of rank is ironic. Whatever the prejudices and preconceptions of readers, *he* will exclude no one from the indictment on account of his rank.

Thus is the pilgrimage revealed as a masquerade. We think we are being offered 'characters' in their habit as they lived. And so we are, down to the very warts on their noses. But the warts in Chaucer are not mere random 'realism'. They are part of a deliberate strategy whereby we do not notice, until it is borne in on us with powerful obliqueness, that we are witnessing, not a depiction of personality, but an unmasking of self—the very inner self. We have our clues in the *Prologue* to warn us of the fact that all is not quite as it seems. In the *Tales*—in those of them at any rate which do seem to be linked to their tellers and their prologues—we have the naked truth. The relationship between tale and teller is not the kind of psychological projection which a modern conception of characterization would demand. The technique is in one sense more primitive than that, akin to the aside or the informative soliloquy of the Elizabethan drama, in which the character unmasks himself (neither wittingly nor unwittingly—his degree of consciousness is irrelevant) in direct revelation to the audience.

It is irony doubly ironic that the master of ceremonies, the critic-unmasker, the poet Chaucer, appears himself masked in the masquerade. Or rather, it is a necessary functional device that he should do so, for his mask of the innocent, the simpleton, is the means whereby he can present in seemingly unsuspecting acceptance, the worldly scale

to be the organizing principle of the *Prologue* and the source of its rich spectrum of values and behaviour, in much the same way as I find Mammon to be. The two views, I think, are complementary.

of values of the pilgrims. He takes them at their face-value, the value they put upon themselves. He is all seriousness. He thinks it a great pity that the Cook has a running sore on his leg; he thinks there is much to be said for the Monk's arguments against Austin; he is sure the Summoner makes a great mistake in underestimating the effectiveness of archdeacons' 'curses'; he finds the Prioress a very pretty lady, and ever so well bred. Only in the case of the Pardoner does he cross the strict bounds of politeness. And little wonder. For the Pardoner stands at the outer pale of Chaucer's tolerance for humanity. He is a concentrate of the maximum rapacity and the maximum hypocrisy. He is parasite of parasites. His tale is the most haunting and powerful of 'moralities'; and its text is *Radix malorum est cupiditas*.

First published in the *Modern Language Review*, Vol. LVIII, (1963), pp. 1–9, and here reprinted by permission of the Editors and the Modern Humanities Research Association.

PAUL RUGGIERS

The Narrator: the Pilgrim as Poet

THE critical loci of the *Canterbury Tales* which must come under
consideration are the *General Prologue*, with its literary apology and
protestations of little wit (ll. 715–24), the *Man of Law's Introduction*,
the conclusion of the *Miller's Prologue* (il. 3167–86), the links fore
and aft of *Sir Thopas*, and of necessity the Retraction. There are
others, but these are the important ones from which we may deduce
something about the character of the pilgrim-poet Chaucer.

For a variety of reasons uniformity of opinion cannot be reached,
one factor being the long evolution of tales, links and *General
Prologue:* perhaps limited freedom for writing spread composition
out over a period of years. The work lacks a single hero steadily in
the foreground who interprets experience. Chaucer himself seems
to be content with letting others dominate the scene, and with letting
their experiences pass before us without that formal control which
other perhaps greater architects like Dante have achieved. It seems to
have been enough to continue the jest, so rich in irony for oral presentation, in which the narrator disavows intelligence of a particular
situation and presents himself from time to time to his audience as
dull and obtuse, lacking knowledge and insight. We have seen Chaucer
create such a persona in the vision poems, and it is possible to trace
out a further development of the persona in the paradox of the
Troilus where the poet's sophistication is contrasted with the
narrator's limited knowledge of love.

The device is useful in the *General Prologue* when the persistent
innocence of the narrator leads to a simpleton's appreciation of the
pilgrims without regard to a common standard of morality, a yielding
to the essential humanity of his companions, a sense of being overwhelmed by their worth, and success, and obvious talents. Praise and
appreciation fall easily from his lips, sometimes for reasons we can
ourselves corroborate, but often with the feeling that the narrator's
personality has led him to equate their worth with their capacity to
arouse interest in him. The candour with which the characters of the
pilgrims are presented allows Chaucer the artist the leeway even of
satire, but Chaucer the persona or pilgrim seems untouched by satirical
intention and is, so to speak, removed from direct attack. Signs of
apparent approval, different in tone from those used to describe the
Knight, Parson, and Plowman, are evident in his praise of the Sum-

moner's good comradeship, of the Pardoner's powers of oratory, of the
Shipman's seamanship, of the Physician's professional skill, of the
Friar's persuasiveness, and of the Monk's prowess as a hunter. Indeed
in such passages as these it is difficult to distinguish in the point of
view of the narrator what is praiseworthy from what is reprehensible.
The effect is one of the most subtle irony in which we can only with
great refinement of thought define the whole range of response: a
charitable appreciation of what is god-like and what is human in men,
a purely secular delight in the great variety within the cooperative
society—these combined in an unusually alert observer of life and in
an unusually astute creator of character. The remarkable reporter
whom the poet has created as Chaucer the pilgrim, without a shred
of malice, has turned out to be his slyest joke.

One can make out a better case for a consistently maintained
persona in the *General Prologue* (though not a thoroughly convincing
one) than one can for the narrator in the remainder of the *Canterbury
Tales*. The apology or defence of literary decorum transcending moral
propriety at the end of the *General Prologue,* with its echo in the
Miller's Prologue where the narrator calls attention to tales dealing
with subjects of morality, religion, and the like, has the knowing air
of containing allusion to the total range of the materials of the *Canterbury Tales,* a foresight that can only be the poet's. There is a sharp
point to the line, 'Blameth nat me if that ye chese amys', which is surely
an ironical aside of the author inviting us to note what is technically
admirable, and not merely a naive remark by a simple narrator.

The Man of Law comments upon Chaucer as a kind of literary
glutton who has used up all the available stories of lovers. He provides
for us a kind of master plan for the *Legend of Good Women* (including
some that never materialize), and exonerates him of writing stories of
incest. Here we have a daring conflation of the real world in which
Chaucer wrote and recited his verses with the world of fiction in which
the pilgrims he has created are able to comment upon that other world
for the sake of some ironic effect which, it is possible, is largely lost to
us now. In this passage of the *Canterbury Tales* fraught with problems, what does emerge is Chaucer's own joke upon himself, imput-
ing to himself, as poet, clumsiness in rhyme and metre (but implying
the opposite), and averring a sense of propriety in subject matter that
may have been placed in doubt by tales already in circulation.

There is more to be assessed in the rich contrast of the two tales
'Chaucer' tells. In *Sir Thopas* and the *Tale of Melibee* we have a
successful and extremely delicate balance between the author in
control of the situation and the narrator with a definite kind of personality, size, and shape who interacts with the other members of the
pilgrimage. There is delicacy too in the jest of offering a bad romance
with such seriousness, a romance which Wells calls a 'scrap of
burlesque'. In the pilgrim-poet's insistence that this is the only tale

in rhyme that he knows, we are a far cry from that Chaucer of the *Man of Law's Introduction* who has apparently had access to many good stories and has used some of them. Somewhat offended by the Host's scurrilous judgment of it (it was the best one he knew), he offers his prose treatise on prudence with apparently the same seriousness of effort, if not of intention, as *Sir Thopas*. Here, more than in the *General Prologue*, we have a convincing and definable personality attributed to the narrator, even when we are not able to recreate the special relationship of poet and audience and the sense of a joke commonly shared. But it is a more subtle jest on a larger scale than that of the *Man of Law's Introduction*, where the enumeration of works accomplished suggests, among other things, a progress report. The difference that we discern may be the result, as we suggested above, of different times of composition.

The problem is further complicated by the emergence of Chaucer's own voice in the Retraction, a voice which must be reckoned with in any estimate of the total effect of the *Canterbury Tales*. In a sense this is the final test of the consistency of the persona-narrator and a gauge of his participation. Some suggestions of this matter I explore later on. Suffice it to say at this time that when the Retraction is spoken, the purely personal moral judgment threatens to shatter the artistry and momentarily to dislocate our values, precisely because it is so personal and unexpected. . . .

One concludes, then, in dealing with the problem of the narrator of the *Canterbury Tales*, that the very character of the medley works against the poet as hero and demands his withdrawal from, rather than his inclusion in, the poem. What we recognize is the absence of the narrator instead of his presence. When he is present he becomes at one extreme a wise simpleton who admires his fellow-man and pleads for the right to describe him honestly, and at the other, an artist concerned with prudence and morality. Indeed, wherever 'Chaucer' appears in his poem, his attitude is that of ironical distance between himself and his audience.

The absence of Chaucer, the persona and poet, as hero of the pilgrimage,[1] obviates the necessity, too, of the personal teacher or guide through whom he gradually achieves God-likeness. Such teachers and guides are to be found, as we have said, in *Pearl*, in the *Confessio Amantis*, and in the *Divine Comedy*. He is, if not the learning hero, the observer and recorder, and through this role we may account for much in the form of the *Canterbury Tales* that provokes and excites us: the discreteness of the fragments, for example, each an island of creative energy with its own cast of characters and inner law; the absence of a single agent on the pilgrimage who interprets each, a deliberate deficiency which enjoins upon the reader the obliga-

---

[1] On the absence of the heroic in late medieval style, see D. W. Robertson, Jr, *A Preface to Chaucer*, p. 285.

H

tion of adding or providing his own experience as the final comment; the generally equitable balance between religious and worldly interests; the implication that the structure of the *Canterbury Tales* could be proliferated at will to include many aspects of experience— these may be taken to corroborate our suggestion that the great middle of the *Canterbury Tales* may successfully be approached as a discursive, even a disjointed, encyclopaedia.

Nonetheless, in terms of its beginning and end, the structure of the *Canterbury Tales* is complete. The fact that the narrator is a withdrawing ironist, not a hero, does not prevent our seeing finally that the society of which he is a part is delivered from its tensions and debates. The pilgrimage theme, with its clear beginning and end, draws even the ironist-narrator into the final 'we' of the audience addressed by the Parson in his attempt to draw together the whole of human society into a pattern of sins and virtues, into confession and repentance. The Retraction offers a final judgment. Its attempt to state the terms of the moral contract in which even artists are involved points to a view of life as well as a literary structure which, by virtue of the hope of redemption with which it closes, must be called Christian and comedic in ultimate intention. . . .

From *The Art of the* 'Canterbury Tales', Madison, University of Wisconsin Press, 1965, pp. 17–23.

WALTER CLYDE CURRY

Chauntecleer and Pertelote on Dreams

An attentive observer of that dispute which arises, in the *Nun's Priest's Tale*, between those tantalizingly human barnyard fowls, Chauntecleer and Pertelote, over the large question of dream-origins, is made to feel that their divergence of opinion grows out of a difference in natural temperament. The controversy is precipitated, it will be recalled, by the necessity of determining to what particular class of dreams the cock's fearful experience of last night belongs before an interpretation of its content can be made. The fair 'damoysele Pertelote', however courteous, debonair, and companionable she may be, is by nature practical of mind and unimaginative; from the top of her coral comb to the tips of her little azure toes she is a scientist, who has peered into many strange corners of medical lore. That egotist, Chauntecleer, imaginative and pompously self-conscious, would like to pass as a philosopher and a deep student of the occult. As might be expected, when they come to classify a particular dream, each does it in accordance with his temperamental and characteristic way of looking at things. And with the perversity of human disputants—I had almost said of some husbands and wives in disagreement—each presents only one aspect of the question, that which appeals to him and with which congenial study has made him most familiar, and ignores practically all other facts which he may know to be true. Pertelote's contentions are well founded when the dream is a *somnium naturale;* Chauntecleer's claims are undeniable when the vision is a true *somnium coeleste.*

Well, as Chauntecleer sits upon his perch one morning with his wives about him, he begins suddenly to groan in his throat as one who is sorely oppressed by some horrible dream. When Pertelote hears him roar, she is aghast. 'O dear heart,' says she, 'what ails you to groan in this manner? For shame, what a sleeper!' And poor Chauntecleer, at last awake and free from his dream, replies: 'By God, madam, I dreamed just now that I was in such trouble that my heart is still terribly frightened. May God interpret my dream aright and keep my body out of prison! It seemed to me that, as I roamed up and down in our yard, I saw a fearful beast something like a dog that attempted to accomplish my death. His colour was between yellow and red; his tail and both his ears were tipped with black; his snout was small, and he had two glowing eyes. Because of his aspect I am still

H*

almost dead with fright. And this, doubtless, was the cause of my groaning.' Pertelote, in some measure the medieval woman, is grievously disappointed at this pitiful spectacle of a strong and, to her, heroic cock torn by so base a thing as fear. 'Alas and wellaway,' she cries, 'fie upon you, chicken-hearted! Now have you lost all my heart and all my love; I cannot love a coward, by my faith. For whatever women may say, we all admire and desire husbands who are hardy, wise, and brave, neither a boaster nor one who is afraid of every little thing. How dare you say in the presence of your love that anything can cause you to fear! Have you, who wear a beard, no man's heart? And worst of all, can you be afraid of a mere dream, which is nothing but vanity?' ...

Then quoting the saying from Cato, *somnia ne cures*—being careful not to mention the other half of what must have been a proverb, *nam fallunt somnia plures*—she advises him to take certain laxatives lest he come down with a tertian fever (*C. T.*, B, 4100–4125).

From all indications it might appear that Pertelote's diagnosis of Chauntecleer's case is about correct; and certainly her presentation of the effects of red and black choler upon the dreaming mind is without fault. It will be seen that she seizes upon the cock's intense fear as a sign of a superabundance of humours in the blood, and in this conclusion she is supported by the best medical opinion. Avicenna, for example, remarks upon the infallible symptoms of melancholia: 'The principal signs of melancholia in the blood are these: fear without cause, swiftness to anger, and trembling; when the humour is strongly established, dread, defective judgment, uneasiness of mind, a kind of apprehension on account of things which are or are not, and for the most part anxiety over that which is not ordinarily feared. Some live in apprehension of robbers, some fear that the earth will open and swallow them, and others that wolves may break in upon them. Sometimes they are terrified at that which comes within the sphere of their activity; at other times they imagine themselves being crowned kings, or transformed into wolves, or into demons, or birds, or even into artificial instruments or implements.'[1]

Chauntecleer's physical condition has not brought him quite to this sad pass, to be sure, but his fears and his dream of a frightful beast are strongly indicative of maladjustment of humours in his system. Up until the moment when his dream is shown by the final outcome to be a prophetic vision, one is inclined to agree with Pertelote's diagnosis, especially so since she is amply supported by the best medical and other authority in her association of Chauntecleer's type of dream with the various complexions. According to Avicenna, for example, one sign of too much choler is a 'dream in which one sees fires, and yellow banners, many other things yellow which are

---

[1] Avicenna, *Libri Canonis quinque*, Venetiis, 1564, lib. III, fen i, tract. 4, cap. 18.

not naturally so, the fervent heat of the bath, or of the sun, and such like', and of *cholera nigra*, 'dreams in which terror is produced from the darkness, by tortures, and by the appearance of black things.'[2] He is supported by Galen, who declares: 'If anyone should see a fire in his dreams, he is troubled by too much yellow bile; if he should see smoke, or misty darkness, or profound shadows, then by black bile';[3] Rhazes is of the opinion that 'when anyone frequently sees fires and lightning and strife in his dreams, red cholera abounds in the blood, but when he beholds many things tinged with a swarthy colour and when he experiences terror and fear, these things signify the working of black cholera'.... The enthusiastic Pertelote knows many more wonders about the effects of humours upon dreams—such as, for example, no doubt, that a super-abundance of blood produces 'dreams in which a man beholds red objects, or much blood flowing from his body, or seems to be swimming in blood', and that excessive phlegm causes 'dreams in which are seen water, rivers, snow and rain, and cold weather'[4]—but she will let that pass (4127ff.). She must hasten on to prescribe a remedy for the malady which she has diagnosed with apparent accuracy and in much detail.

Chauntecleer's affection as indicated by his fear and the dream must be rigorously attacked before it has had time to develop into something more dangerous; and Pertelote's proposed method of procedure is worthy of the wisest medical men. This busy little housewife, in real concern for the health of her lord and husband—and perhaps eager to show him that, for once, in spite of her femininity she is not so ignorant and incapable as might be supposed—counsels that forthwith and immediately steps be taken to purge this choler and melancholy (4132–7). Because there is no apothecary in that town, she herself will teach him the properties of all the herbs in their yard which are by nature useful in purging humours, both above and below. 'Beware,' she warns, 'that the sun in his ascension does not find you still replete with hot humours—you are very choleric of complexion—lest you be afflicted with a tertian fever or an ague, which may prove your destruction.' For a day or two at first he shall have digestives of worms before he takes his laxatives of *laurus, centauria, fumaria, elleborus, euphorbium, rhamus,* and *hedera helix.* He must

> Pekke hem up right as they growe, and ete hem in.
>
> (*C. T.,* B, 4140–57).

Evidently Pertelote has been reading after the physicians. They all understand that it is not safe to administer purgatives or laxatives for hot humours until after 'digestives', i.e., medicines for absorbing or dissipating melancholy and choler, have been given for some time.

---

[2] *Ibid.,* lib. I, fen 2, doc. 3, cap. 7.
[3] *Opera,* Venetiis, 1609, VI, 213.
[4] Avicenna, *op. cit.,* lib. I, fen 2, doc. 3, cap. 7.

118 CRITICS ON CHAUCER

Richard Saunders, in *The Astrological Judgment and Practice of Physic*, requires several pages upon which to record the best digestives of these humours—though, of course, he has nothing to say about 'digestyves of wormes'! And the little hen is wise in her selection of simples. Dioscorides—Chaucer's 'Deiscorides' (*C. T.*, A. 430)—says of *laurus noblis* ('lauriol') that 'when taken in water it sits heavy on the stomach and incites vomiting'; of *centauria*, 'It expels bilious and heavy humours through the bowels'; of *fumaria* or *fumus terre* ('fumetere'), 'This herb consumed in food induces bilious urine'; of black *elleborus* ('ellebor'), 'It purges through the lower tracts both phlegm and choleric humours, when given by itself or with scarmonia; it is good for epileptics, mad men, and for those afflicted with melancholia and nervousness'; of *euphorbium* ('catapuce'), 'It is a continuous irritant having power to dissipate the suffusion of noxious humours'; of *rhamus* ('gaytres beryis'), 'When placed in the doors and windows the branches of this herb are said to repel the evil influences of magicians'; and of *hedera helix* ('erbe yve'), 'All species of ivy are acrid, astringent, and particularly effective in cases of nervousness.'[5] Surely after Chauntecleer has taken any small part of this prescription to purge him above and below, he will be in dire need of the *hedera helix*. But it is only by such an heroic course of action that fevers and agues may be avoided.

Pertelote is, moreover, quite right again when she informs her dear husband that the corruption of red and black choler in the blood causes intermittent fevers and rigors. Having decided that red choler especially is at the bottom of Chauntecleer's trouble (4118), she arrives at the logical and scientific conclusion that his fever will be tertian. Avicenna would pronounce her deductions correct. He observes that there are in general two species of fevers, *febres aegritudines* and *febres accidentes*, with the latter of which he would identify the *febris putredinis*.[6] (We are not concerned with the *febris apostematis*, which is also classified under *accidentis*.) Now this *febris putredinis* is so named because it results from a corruption of the four humours of the body, giving rise, in consequence, to four different kinds of fevers, namely, *tertiana, quartana, quotidiana,* and *continua* (which must not be confused with the *febres accidentes*, all continuous). 'The corruption of cholera produces the *tertiana;* the corruption of melancholia, the *quartana;* of phlegm, the *quotidiana;* and the corruption of blood, the *continua.*'[7] Of these we are interested only in the *tertiana*, which

---

[5] Pedanii Dioscoridis Anazarbei, *De materia medica libri quinque*, ed. Springel in *Opera quae extant*, I: *laurus*, lib. I, cap. 106; *centauria*, cap. 7; *fumaria*, cap. 108; *elleborus*, cap. 149; *euphorbium*, cap. 86; *rhamus*, cap. 119; *hedera helix*, cap. 210. For further quotations from Avicenna, see *Englische Studien*, LVIII, p. 49.

[6] *Op. cit.*, lib. IV, fen 1, tract. 1, cap. i.

[7] *Ibid.*, lib. IV, fen 1, tract. 2, cap. i.

may be the result of *cholera pura* or *non pura*, i.e., unmixed or mixed with other humours. Of the *tertiana* type, therefore, there are at least three kinds, *tertiana continua, tertiana periodica,* and *causon* (or *febris ardens*).[8] The *periodica*, being the result of corrupted *cholera pura*, is mild and easily controlled; but the other two, since before the patient can recover from one attack another paroxysm is upon him, are more violent and usually accompanied by agues. It is possibly to one of these that Pertelote refers, most likely to the *causon*, because as we have seen in Chauntecleer's case red choler is supposed to be mixed with black choler, or melancholia. Avicenna describes the symptoms of an attack: 'A paroxysm of tertian fever begins with a kind of goose-flesh sensation as if the skin were being pricked with the point of a hot needle; then a sudden chill descends upon the patient attended by rigors, each one of which becomes harder than that before. And during the first three days of the fever's course these rigors are strongest and most vahement.'[9] One may expect the progress of the malady to run as follows: 'First there is felt the prickling sensation mentioned above, then the chill and the rigor; afterwards the rigor moderates and the chill abates, and fever begins; this state continues for awhile; and after that the fever gradually diminishes until it disappears altogether.'[10] Indeed, if Chauntecleer's dream were caused by the corruption of red and black choler in the blood—and Pertelote seems to have made out an excellent case—it would be foolish for him to carry his hot humours into the sunshine.

Against Pertelote's presentation of scientifically accurate facts and sound medical theory, Chauntecleer has nothing to oppose but his colossal conceit and a few stories gleaned from old authorities. His manly self-love must have writhed under the lash of his little wife's outspoken contempt for his fears at so paltry a thing as a dream caused by choler. Still, assuming a lordly air of condescension—as no doubt befits a husband when confronted by unanswerable arguments—the cock proceeds to shift the basis of the discussion from fact to authority. 'Madam,' says he, 'I have great respect for your knowledge. But as for this Cato with his *somnia ne cures*, let me inform you that many men of vastly more authority than ever Cato was have held the reverse of his opinion and have found by experience that dreams are significant as presagers of future joy and tribulation.' (4160–70).

> Ther nedeth make of this noon argument;
> The verray preve sheweth it in dede   (4172).

As a matter of fact, never having thought independently for himself, Chauntecleer has no conception of what rightly constitutes a proof. For all his show of scholarly learning and for all his evident desire to pass

---

[8] *Ibid.*, lib. IV, fen 1, tract. 2, cap. 35.
[9] *Ibid.*, lib. IV, fen 1, tract. 2, cap. 36.
[10] *Ibid.*, lib. IV, fen 1, tract. 1, cap. 4.

as a widely read and deep student of the occult, he has never investig-
ated the philosophy or the psychology of dreams. His puerile mind
is capable of grasping only the thread of a marvellous story, trusting
blindly and with childlike simplicity to the correctness of interpreta-
tions offered by authorities. He impresses his audience with the narration of two stories from 'oon of the gretteste auctours that men rede'—
being careful not to mention Cicero as the author, probably because
he does not know—in which certain events perceived in dreams come
true precisely as visualized in sleep (4175-4294). He is copious in
detail and points with pedantic pride to the exact book and chapter
where one of the stories may be found, but he has no way of determining whether such dreams—which belong to the type *somnium
animale*—are to be considered more credible than the true revelations which he mentions later. With blithe unconsciousness of any
fundamental difference, he lumps them all together. He has read and
enjoyed immensely the fulfilled 'avisioun' of St Kenelm—he was the
son of Kenulphus, King of Mercia, be it known!—and in the Old
Testament the dream of Daniel (4319) and of Joseph (4320) and of the
King of Egypt (4323), all of which proved to be significant. He
recalls that Croesus—who was the King of Lydia—was warned in a
dream that he should be hanged (4328), and that Andromache—she
was Hector's wife—saw in a vision precisely how her husband
should be slain at the hands of Achilles (4330). The testimony of
Macrobius as to the validity of dreams is presented (4314), though
complete silence is observed regarding this same Macrobius's *insomnium* and *phantasma*. At any rate, before the overwhelmed little hen
can speak what may be in her mind—one may suspect that she smiles
behind her wing—her erudite husband proceeds to close the argument
to his complete satisfaction with a bit of flattery and with the assurance
that, since events have followed upon the dreams of these other great
men, his own 'avisioun' will surely be fulfilled in adversity (4341).
Besides, he sets no store by these laxatives; they are venomous and
nauseous; he defies the whole prescription (4345).

It is entirely characteristic of Chauntecleer to classify his dream as
an 'avisioun'. Common, ordinary men may experience such dreams as
the *somnium naturale,* or the *insomnium* or the *phantasma,* but most
of the fulfilled dreams recorded by the authorities have been authentic
visiones, or divine revelations granted to famous men, illustrious
warriors, mighty kings of nations, prophets, seers. Why should the cock
be considered—in his own estimation—less worthy than these to
receive an 'avisioun'? Still, the fact remains, as Antonius Gaizo
observes regarding the dreams recorded by Valerius Maximus, that
'those visions which may be called celestial are most rare, and are not
granted except to great men. But because such are sometimes significant no one ought, therefore, to identify himself with that class of men
who persuade themselves that they should put faith in their own

somnia naturalia or *animalia*.[11] Granting, however, the authenticity of Chauntecleer's 'avisioun', one need experience no surprise at his impudent disregard of its apparent warning. In the full joy of conscious strength he flies from the beams as usual, thinking no doubt that, though these other great ones might have been controlled by the fate revealed in dreams, one so powerful and favoured as he may surely escape. That is Chauntecleer!

Evidently the mind of this self-satisfied personage has never attacked the problem of 'necessity' in its relation to foreknowledge as revealed in the *somnium coeleste*. Consequently, since the cock has made so poor a showing as a philosopher and theologian, the Nun's Priest feels called upon to broach the subject at least in direct connection with Chauntecleer's 'avisioun'. 'Alas,' says he in mock-heroic vein,

> O Chauntecleer, accursed be that morwe
> That thou into the yerd flough fro the bemes!
> Thou were ful y-warned by thy dremes,
> That thilke day was perilous to thee,
> But what god forwoot mot nedes be,
> After the opinioun of certeyn clerkis.
>
> (*C. T.*, B, 4420 ff.)

He cannot settle the question, upon which there has been altercation by an hundred thousand men, as to whether God's foreknowledge of coming events constrains a man by 'simple necessitee' or whether the power of choice residing in human free-will may alter such constraint into 'necessitee condicionel'. Happily this writer is also spared the task of solving the problem; Augustine, and Professor Carlton Brown, and Boethius, and Professor J. S. P. Tatlock, and Bishop Bradwardine, and Professor H. R. Patch have already 'bulted it to the bren'.[12] It may be noted in passing, however, that in showing how Grosseteste solves the general problem of foreknowledge and free-will through the postulation of two kinds of necessity, *antecedentis* ('simple necessitee') and *contingentia* ('necessitee condicionel'), Bradwardine applies the same method to the relation of necessity to foreknowledge as made patent in *revelations*. 'In the same way,' he concludes, 'may be solved the problem of free-will in relation to the foreknowledge of the prophet. For the whole question of why these seem to be mutually

---

[11] Gaizo, *De somno ac eius necessitate*, Basillae, 1539, cap. vii. For the sources of the cock's illustrations, see Cicero, *De divinatione*, lib. I, cap. 27; Valerius Maximus, *Factorum et Dictorum memorabilium libri novem*, lib. I, cap. vii. Cf. Lounsbury, II, 272.

[12] Bradwardine, *De Causa Dei*, ed. Savillius, London, 1618, pp. 810–12; Augustine, *De Civitate Dei*, cap. 14; Boethius, *De consolatione philosophiae*, V, 6: C. F. Brown, 'The Author of the *Pearl* Considered in the Light of his Theological Opinions,' *PMLA.*, XIX, 265; H. R. Patch, 'Troilus on Predestination,' *JEGPh.*, XVII, 399 ff.; Wedel, *The Medieval Attitude toward Astrology*, pp. 147–149; *Die Philosophischen Werke des Robert Grosseteste*, ed. Bauer, pp. 158–60.

contradictory, so that they cannot exist at the same time, is none other than that one is contingent and possible whichever way you look at it, and the other is absolutely necessary and seems not to allow of any contingency in that which follows. A thing that is foreknown is possible from any point of view. The foreknowledge of a thing, when it actually is, cannot be otherwise than it is. Hence it is necessary that knowledge be perfected by that which follows, even though that which is to follow is for the time being contingent. Thus contingent necessity, as has been said, does not seem to permit antecedent necessity, but to contradict it.[13] One may conclude, therefore, that if Chauntecleer had ever taken the trouble to learn the distinction between simple and conditional necessity and if his mind had been less obsessed with the idea of his own importance, the fulfilment of even so true an 'avisioun' as his might have been averted by the mere expedient of remaining upon the beams.

In the *Nun's Priest's Tale* Chaucer has given an excellent demonstration of how the true artist may use scientific and philosophical material in the development of his characters. Nearly half the space compassed by the story is devoted to the controversy over dreams, but by the end of it the reader is fairly well acquainted with Chauntecleer and Pertelote and is ready to accept the ensuing action in which they play their parts. While the discussion is staged, of course, for the sole purpose of developing these characters, still it *seems* as if the divergence of opinion arises naturally out of a fundamental difference in temperament. Hence the reader forgets for the time being that Chaucer is perhaps deliberately manufacturing a situation peopled by creatures of his imagination, and suffers himself to rest under the illusion that he is beholding the expression of personality in action as in real life. And the creation and maintenance of this illusion, I take it, is art. . . .

From *Chaucer and the Medieval Sciences,* Oxford, 1926; revised edition, Allen and Unwin, 1960, pp. 219–232.

[13] *Op. cit.,* p. 811.

CHARLES MUSCATINE

Form, Texture and Meaning in Chaucer's *Knight's Tale*

... When we look at the poem's structure, we find symmetry to be its
most prominent feature. By 'symmetry' I do not mean 'unity', but
rather, a high degree of regularity and order among parts. The poem
does fulfil our demand for unity; however, it is not unity in itself, but
unity through regularity that has particular meaning in the *Knight's
Tale*.

The character-grouping is symmetrical. There are two knights,
Palamon and Arcite, in love with the same woman, Emilye. Above
the three and in a position to sit in judgment, is the Duke Theseus,
who throughout the poem is the centre of authority and the balance
between the opposing interests of the knights. In the realm of the
supernatural, each of the knights and the lady has a patron deity:
Venus, Mars, and Diana. The conflict between Venus and Mars is
resolved by the elder Saturn, with no partiality toward either. In the
tournament each knight is accompanied by one hundred followers,
headed by a particularly notable king, on one side Lygurge, on the
other Emetrius:

> In al the world, to seken up and doun,
> So evene, withouten variacioun,
> Ther nere swiche compaignyes tweye;
> For ther was noon so wys that koude seye
> That any hadde of oother avauntage
> Of worthynesse, ne of estaat, ne age,
> So evene were they chosen, for to gesse.
> And in two renges faire they hem dresse.

This arrangement of the two companies *in two renges* is one of
many details of symmetry of scene and action in the poem. At the very
beginning of the poem we find a uniformly clad company 'of ladyes,
tweye and tweye,/Ech after oother'. When Palamon and Arcite are
found in the heap of bodies by Thebes, they are 'ligynge by and by,/
Booth in oon armes'. We find that they are cousins, 'of sustren two
yborn'.

In the scene following the discovery of Emilye, each offers a lyric on
the subject. When Arcite is released from prison, each delivers a
complaint in which even the vocabulary and theme are symmetrical:

> 'O deere cosyn Palamon,' quod he,
> 'Thyn is the victorie of this aventure.'

'Allas,' quod he, 'Arcita, cosyn myn,
Of al oure strif, God woot, the fruyt is thyn.'

In part two, the narrator divides his attention between them, in altern-
ate descriptions; and in the fight subsequent to their meeting, they are
evenly matched:

Thou myghtest wene that this Palamon
In his fightyng were a wood leon,
And as a crueel tigre was Arcite. . . .

Theseus appears, 'And at a stert he was bitwix hem two.' He sets
the conditions of the tournament in round numbers: 'And this day
fifty wykes, fer ne ner/Everich of you shal brynge an hundred knightes.
. . . .' In the third part the narrator describes the making of lists, in the
same place as where the first fight occurs. The lists are circular in
shape, a mile in circumference. They are entered from east and
west by identical marble gates. The altars or temples of Mars and
Venus are situated above these gates. Northward (and equidistant from
the other two, no doubt) is the *oratorie* of Diana. The three temples are
described in succession, and each description is subdivided in the same
way: first the wall-painting with its allegorical figures, and then the
statue of the deity itself.

The symmetry of description continues with parallel accounts of the
two rival companies, each containing a portrait of the leading king. Then
follow the prayers of the principals: Palamon to Venus, Emilye to
Diana, Arcite to Mars. The prayers are made at the hours dedicated by
astrology to those deities, and each prayer is answered by some supernatural event. Internally, too, the three prayers show a striking similarity of design, each beginning with rhetorical *pronominatio*, and
continuing with a reference to the deity's relations with the opposite
sex, a self-description by the speaker, a humble assertion of incompet-
ence, a request for assistance, and a promise to worship. The spectators
enter the lists and are seated in order of rank. The combatants, Palamon
and Arcite, with banners white and red respectively, enter the field
through the gates of Venus and Mars.

After Arcite's death, his sepulchre is described. It is erected 'ther
as first Arcite and Palamoun/Hadden for love the bataille hem
bitwene'. As R. A. Pratt notes, this is also where the lists were built.[1]
The funeral procession, like the procession to the lists, is character-
ized by precise order, and the details of the funeral are full of the
same kind of ordering:

. . . the Grekes, with an huge route,
Thries riden al the fyr aboute
Upon the left hand, with a loud shoutynge,
And thries with hir speres claterynge;
And thries how the ladys gonne crye . . .

[1] 'Chaucer's Use of the *Teseida*', P.M.L.A., vol. LXII, (1947), 615, n.60.

Further elements in the poem's symmetry of structure and scene could readily be brought forward.

Turning now from structure to pace, we find the *Tale* deliberately slow and majestic. Random references to generous periods of time make the story chronologically slow. Though Chaucer omits a great deal of the tale originally told by Boccaccio in the *Teseida,* he frequently resorts to the rhetorical device of *occupatio* to summarize in detail events or descriptions in such a way as to shorten the story without losing its weight and impressiveness. Further, there is an extraordinary amount of direct description in the poem, all of which slows the narrative. The description of the lists is very detailed, and placed so as to give the impression that we are present at their construction, an operation that appears to consume the full fifty weeks that Theseus allows for it. The narrator's repetitious 'saugh I', and his closing remark, 'Now been thise lystes maad', cooperate to this effect.

We can hardly fail to note, too, that a great deal of this descriptive material has a richness of detail far in excess of the demands of the story. At first glance, at least, many passages appear to be irrelevant and detachable. To take a well-known instance, we have sixty-one lines of description of Emetrius and Lygurge; yet so far as the action of the poem is concerned, these two worthies do practically nothing.

Like the descriptions and narrator's comments, the direct discourse in the *Tale* contributes to the poem's slowness. There is virtually no rapid dialogue. Speeches of twenty-five or thirty lines are the rule, and one, the final oration of Theseus, is over a hundred lines in length. More than length, however, the non-dynamic *quality* of the speeches is characteristic of the whole poem's style. Many of them have only a nominal value as action, or the instruments to action. Formal, rhetorical structure, and a function comparatively unrelated to the practical necessities of the dramatic situation, are the rule. This is true even where the speech is addressed to another character. For instance, when old Saturn is badgered by his granddaughter Venus to aid her in her conflict with Mars, he replies as follows:

> 'My deere doghter Venus,' quod Saturne,
> 'My cours, that hath so wyde for to turne,
> Hath moore power than woot any man.
> Myn is the drenchyng in the see so wan;
> Myn is the prisoun in the derke cote,
> Myn is the stranglyng and hangyng by the throte,
> The murmure and the cherles rebellyng,
> The groynynge, and the pryvee empoysonyng;
> I do vengeance and pleyn correccioun,
> Whil I dwelle in the signe of the leoun,
> Myn is the ruyne of the hye halles,
> The fallynge of the toures and of the walles
> Upon the mynour or the carpenter.
> I slow Sampsoun, shakynge the piler;

I

And myne be the maladyes colde,
The derke tresons, and the castes olde;
My lookyng is the fader of pestilence.
Now weep namoore, I shal doon diligence. . . .'

And finally, the remainder of the speech, a mere eight lines, is
devoted to promising Venus his aid. We can safely assume that Venus
knows all about her grandfather. The long, self-descriptive introduction, therefore, must have some function other than the dramatic.

Going on now to the nature of the action, we find that, while the
chivalric aspects of the scene are described with minute particularity,
there is very little in the *Knight's Tale* of the intimate and distinctive
details of look, attitude, and gesture that mark some of Chaucer's more
naturalistic poems. The *Tale* is replete with conventional stage
business. There are swoons and cries, fallings on knees, and sudden
palenesses; there is a symphony of howls, wails and lamentations.

These general and inescapable observations on the nature of the
Knight's Tale make clear how the poem must be approached. The
symmetry of scene, action and character-grouping, the slow pace of
the narrative and large proportion of concrete description, the predominantly lyric and philosophic kind of discourse—along with a lack of
subtle discrimination in the stage business—all indicate that the tale
is not the best kind in which to look for either delicate characterization
or the peculiar fascination of an exciting plot.

Chaucer's modifications of the *Teseida* all seem to bear this out. He
found much of his material in the long Italian work. By selection and
addition he produced a poem much more symmetrical than its source.
Chaucer even regularizes the times and places of the incidents in
Boccaccio, and many further instances of an increase in symmetry
could be cited. The crowning modification, however, is the equalization
of Palamon and Arcite. We have seen that this has caused some
consternation in the critical ranks. It should now be clear that the
critic is not on safe ground when he calls this lack of characterization
the story's greatest weakness. The point is rather that subtle delinea-
tion of character is neither called for in the poem's design nor possible of achievement through the technical means Chaucer largely
employs. There is neither rapid dialogue, nor psychological analysis,
nor delicate and revelatory 'business' in the poem. The general intention indicated by the poem's materials and structure lies in a different
direction.

But to recognize that the element of characterization is justly minor
in the tale does not justify turning to the plot, and making it, in turn,
the centre of interest. For the fact is that even as bare plots go, as story
interest goes, the *Knight's Tale* does not amount to much. The value
of the poem depends little on the virtues that make a good story: a
swift pace, suspense, variety, intrigue. Its main events are forecast long
before they occur. The structure of the poem, indeed, works against

story interest. Symmetry in character-grouping, movement, time and place supports the leisurely narrative and description in producing an over-all sense of rest and deliberateness.

With these traditional possibilities eliminated, and under the principle that a poem should be read on the basis of its own assumptions, it seems reasonable to conclude that the *Knight's Tale* is of a kind having a much closer affinity to the medieval tradition of conventionalism than to realism. We can neither examine nor evaluate it according to canons by which it patently was not written and could never satisfy. Its texture reminds one more of the *Roman de la Rose* than of the *General Prologue*. Its grouping and action, rather than existing for any great interest in themselves, seem constantly to point to a non-representational, metaphorical method. Indeed, there is such a close correlation among all its elements on this level as to give decisive support to such an approach.

I would suggest, then, that the *Knight's Tale* is essentially neither a story, nor a static picture, but a poetic pageant, and that all its materials are organized and contributory to a complex design expressing the nature of the noble life,

> That is to seyn, trouthe, honour, kynghthede,
> Wysdom, humblesse, estaat, and heigh kynrede,
> Fredom, and al that longeth to that art. . . .

The story is immediately concerned with those two noble activities, love and chivalry, but even more important is the general tenor of the noble life, the pomp and ceremony, the dignity and power, and particularly the repose and assurance with which the exponent of nobility invokes order. Order, which characterizes the framework of the poem, is also the heart of its meaning. The society depicted is one in which form is full of significance, in which life is conducted at a dignified, professional pace, and wherein life's pattern is itself a reflection, or better, a reproduction, of the order of the universe. And what gives this conception of life its perspective, its depth and seriousness, is its constant awareness of a formidably antagonistic element—chaos, disorder—which in life is an ever-threatening possibility, even in the moment of supremest assuredness, and which in the poem falls across the pattern of order, being clearly exemplified in the erratic reversals of the poem's plot, and deeply embedded in the poem's texture. . . .

On the walls of the temple of Diana are depicted the stories of Callisto, Daphne, Actaeon, and Meleager, all of unhappy memory. In the description of Mars' temple, the narrator is most powerful. He sees

> . . . the derke ymaginyng
> Of Felonye, and all the compassyng;
> The crueel Ire, reed as any gleede;
> The pykepurs, and eek the pale Drede;

128   CRITICS ON CHAUCER

> The smylere with the knyf under the cloke;
> The shepne brennynge with the blake smoke;
> The tresoun of the mordrynge in the bedde;
> The open werre, with woundes al bibledde. . . .

In this context, the monologue of Saturn is the culminating expression of an ever-swelling undertheme of disaster:

> 'Myn is the drenchyng in the see so wan;
> Myn is the prisoun in the derke cote,
> Myn is the stranglyng and hangyng by the throte,
> The murmure and the cherles rebellyng,
> The groynynge, and the pryvee empoysonyng. . . .'

In Theseus' majestic summary there is a final echo, the continuing rhetorical repetition as insistent as fate itself:

> 'He moot be deed, the kyng as shal a page;
> Som in his bed, som in the depe see,
> Som in the large feeld, as men may see. . . .'

This subsurface insistence on disorder is the poem's crowning complexity, its most compelling claim to maturity. We have here no glittering, romantic fairy-castle world. The impressive, patterned edifice of the noble life, its dignity and richness, its regard for law and decorum, are all bulwarks against the ever-threatening forces of chaos, and in constant collision with them. And the crowning nobility, as expressed by this poem, goes beyond a grasp of the forms of social and civil order, beyond magnificence in any earthly sense, to a perception of the order beyond chaos. When the earthly designs suddenly crumble, true nobility is faith in the ultimate order of all things. Saturn, disorder, nothing more or less, is the agent of Arcite's death, and Theseus, noble in the highest sense, interprets it in the deepest perspective. In contrast is the incomplete perception of the wailing women of Athens:

> 'Why woldestow be deed,' thise wommen crye,
> And haddest gold ynough, and Emelye?'

The history of Thebes had perpetual interest for Chaucer as an example of the struggle between noble designs and chaos. Palamon and Arcite, Thebans, lovers, fighters and sufferers, through whom the pursuit of the noble life is presented, exemplify through their experiences and express through their speeches this central conflict.

Reprinted by permission of the Modern Language Association of America from *Proceedings of the Modern Language Association*, vol. 65, 1950, pp. 911–29. It also appears in *Chaucer: Modern Essays in Criticism* (ed. Wagenknecht). New York and Oxford 1959, pp. 64–81. Five footnotes have been omitted.

G. H. GEROULD

The Vicious Pardoner

... The commentators who have urged that his discourse is patterned
on the conventional sermon of the medieval period, with the tale itself
serving as the customary *exemplum*, have encountered very serious
difficulties. Granted that the Pardoner is a creature of unexampled
effrontery, he is by his own account and by the evidence of his performance a gifted pulpit orator. If he were bent on preaching a sermon or
even making an impudent burlesque of one, he surely would have been
able to give it a satisfactory formal arrangement, or Chaucer would
have done so for him. Yet he follows no plan. He does not even move
forward, but instead rambles from topic to topic as one thing suggests
another. He begins by saying that avarice is his sole theme as a preacher,
but he deserts it at once for his confession and returns to it only to
emphasize his own wickedness. He recalls his engagement to tell a
story, but drops the tale after a few lines and drifts into a denuncia-
tion first of gluttony and then of gambling. This is no illustration of
medieval sermonizing, though the speaker is a trained preacher and
incidentally displays both knowledge of homiletic materials and tricks
of his profession.

Nor will the Pardoner's impudent rascality explain his tirade. A
man so depraved and so intent on getting for himself every possible
creature comfort would not, unless his natural inhibitions were suspended, have stripped himself naked in mixed company. He would have
been too canny for that. His loss of control, and therefore his whole
performance, can be explained only by understanding that he was tipsy,
and tipsy to the point of not caring what he said and indeed not
being altogether conscious of it. No cup or two of ale at a wayside
tavern would have brought him to the state which Chaucer suggests
with such marvellous skill. Drink has not only loosened his tongue, as
has sometimes been admitted by critics, but it has thoroughly befud-
dled him.

When he comes at length to the point of telling his 'moral tale',
Chaucer as is wholly right takes over. He could not, and did not, let
any hint of drunken buffoonery mar the grim and tragic irony of the
narrative. To that end he sacrificed dramatic propriety. At least he did
so if we regard the surface only. The Pardoner could not give the
story the form it has, or the moral force. He would spoil the tale if it
were delivered in the vein proper to him. Yet as shaped by Chaucer

—as all the tales really are, of course—the dramatic irony of its attribution to the Pardoner is not lost. In his soberer hours that 'ful vicious man', who was nevertheless intelligent, might well have appreciated this.

What I am not wise enough to explain satisfactorily is how Chaucer shifted the tone from dramatic verisimilitude to dramatic formalism without breaking the continuity. It is the voice of the Pardoner which goes on, but of a Pardoner cleansed and elevated. There are the same sharply outlined images, the same verse rhythms accommodated to natural speech at one point and raised to passionate utterance at another. The tale does not clash with what has gone before. Yet much of its power lies in the restraint with which terrible events are chronicled and in the beautiful precision of their inexorable movement. It could not be more different in these respects from the scrambled tirade by which it is preceded. The skill with which the two are adapted to one another without sacrificing their individual qualities is beyond praise.

There is little need any longer to stress the merits of the narrative attributed to the Pardoner. Everyone knows its transcendent worth: the compression and understatement by which the tensity of mood is maintained; the irony by which the three searchers for the pleasures of life find death, while the old man who may be Death himself cannot escape a semblance of life; the sense of mystery, which is the mystery of fate and free-will. It is great because it has a meaning beyond its immediate meaning.

As I have already said, the scene in the Flanders tavern can have nothing whatever to do with the tale of the three rioters in search of death, and the attempt to connect the two is futile. The tavern in Flanders is riotously gay, filled with young folk who indulge in every kind of folly. There are also the attendants, the sellers of food and drink, the entertainers, and the providers of entertainment. The house must have been very full. In contrast, the other tavern is a melancholy place, deserted by everyone except the host, a boy, and the three lonely customers. It is early morning in a time of pestilence, and the three men have settled down to drink but not in a spirit of gaiety, we are certain. The air is heavy with evil portent, and the mood is not lightened when the corpse of an old acquaintance is carried by. No two scenes could be more different than this and that. Critics have been led astray, no doubt, by the abruptness with which the Pardoner begins his story of the search for death.

> Thise riotoures thre of whiche I telle,

he says, though there has been no previous mention of them. The phrase 'of whiche I telle' refers, of course, to the present and the future and not to the past, and it serves as a link with the preceding anecdote of the quarrelsome gamesters.

At the end of the tale the Pardoner may be said to resume his discourse in person, for Chaucer no longer orders and restrains the wild torrent of his eloquence. Though the tale has taken the place of the customary *exemplum* in what the Pardoner by this time seems to have come momentarily to regard as a sermon, it interrupts his personal performance, which has turned out to be confessional. And now he is at his histrionic but slightly incoherent best. (895)

> O cursed synne of alle cursednesse!
> O traytours homycide, O wikkednesse!
> O glotonye, luxurie, and hasardrye!
> Thou blasphemour of Crist with vileynye
> And othes grete, of usage and of pride!

This is the rhetoric of the spell-binder to whom sense matters little if the sound is right. It is so earnest in tone that one might almost believe the speaker to be self-convinced. Self-forgetful to the extent of being lost in his part we must certainly believe him to be, else he would not go on to attempt the sale of his pardons. He had adequately explained their nature. Now he wishes to free his auditors from the sin of avarice, which is a return to the theme with which he began.

Then his intoxication, whether with ale or with his own acting, appears suddenly to end. 'And lo, sires, thus I preche,' he says flatly, and goes on in three lines (916–918) to speak for the first time like an honest man.

> And Jhesu Crist, that is oure soules leche,
> So graunte yow his pardoun to receyve,
> For that is best; I wol yow nat deceyve.

These are words of truth and soberness, and puzzling words to be spoken by the Pardoner as he has revealed himself. In spite of their difficulty, however, we should be unwise to assume that they are 'out of character'. The Pardoner is Chaucer's creation, and everyone recognizes him to be a very great fictional creation. His unexpected and momentary exhibition of decency must be accepted without reserve, since his author attributed it to him. We may speculate as much as we please about this white spot on his cloak of infamy, but we cannot escape it. Just there, briefly, the Pardoner showed that he knew the difference between good and evil, between truth and falsehood. One may guess that Chaucer put the words in his mouth because he meant him to be a human being. He was a very wicked man, but no devil.

His immediate return thereafter to cynical effrontery is what one would expect, for such effrontery is his habitual mood. Sobered, and no doubt conscious of his self-betrayal, he becomes more impudent than ever in offering his unholy wares for sale. Perhaps there is mockery in his most blasphemous proposal of all:

Or elles taketh pardoun as ye wende,
Al newe and fressh at every miles ende,

but mockery would make it no less odious. In retrospect, or regarded
as a fictional character, the Pardoner is so amusing that he fails to
shock us by his wickedness. His immediate effect would inevitably be
different. Otherwise the Host would not have flared into such hot
anger when the Pardoner suggested that he be the first to get a pardon
as the one 'moost envoluped in synne'. The utter grossness of his
retort is the measure of his disgust at the Pardoner's brazen hypocrisy.
One cannot suppose that Harry Bailly would ordinarily have been so
sensitive about a reference to his human frailties, but his wrath on this
occasion is understandable. It would have been like being attacked
by a rat. The Pardoner's speechless anger when flooded by the Host's
obscenity is also easy to understand. Only by the intervention of the
Knight could peace be restored. . . .

From *Chaucerian Essays*, Princeton University Press, 1952,
pp. 66–71.

W. W. LAWRENCE

The *Tale of Melibeus*

... The truth is that just those qualities in this long piece which we find tedious were highly esteemed in the Middle Ages. If we imagine it freed from all that bores us, there would not be much left. But, since it affected our forefathers so differently, it offers an unrivalled opportunity for studying changes in literary taste, for contrasting medieval and modern conceptions of what makes profitable reading. To this even the elementary student and the 'general reader' should give some attention today. They cannot be expected to plough through the whole of the *Melibeus,* but they should be reminded that they must read not only what diverts them, but what does not, if they really wish to know Chaucer and to understand the significance of his work for the days in which it was written. The very fact that the *Melibeus* lacks interest should stimulate interest to find out why this is so.

This pursuit would be more entertaining, though less instructive, if Chaucer had put something of himself into the tale. His version is a close translation of a French condensation of the *Liber Consolationis et Consilii* of Albertanus of Brescia, written in 1246, but he was also familiar with the Latin. ...

Much of the fascination which the *Melibeus* held for medieval readers lay, of course, in its pervading didacticism, and its wise saws drawn from past authorities and from current tradition. Times have changed; sustained moralizing is repellent to us today. We are absorbed in concrete issues; we believe that we enjoy an advanced civilization, and yet that the world is changing so rapidly that the past is no guide for its problems. The Middle Ages, as every one knows, felt otherwise. Where we look forward to new ideologies, new 'deals', new principles of government and justice, they looked backward in the confident trust that earlier and happier times could best teach them how to live. They were conscious of being in a world not yet reduced to order, and were eager to get it arranged according to the most approved moral principles. In criticizing the *Melibeus,* Professor Tatlock has emphasized their 'perpetual relish in the gnomic style', and pointed out how frequently Chaucer employed it and how much he obviously enjoyed it. Furthermore, 'the interest of the earlier Middle Ages in creative literature has been chiefly for lyric feeling and for action; they had produced little analysis of human motive and shown little knowledge of the human heart. At a certain stage in the intellectual development of a people, these become intelligible and attractive;

witness the rise of literary allegory into popularity in the thirteenth century. Now *Melibeus* offers both; strange as the statement may seem at first, *Melibeus* really shows insight.'[1] With this I am quite in agreement, and I wish that Professor Tatlock had further developed this point. But I think that another and more important feature of the tale has been strangely neglected—its repeated and earnest pleading for peace rather than war, for mediation and law rather than private revenge. Compared with this, its moral lessons, its psychologizing, and its elegant extracts seem of secondary significance.

... the shortcomings of the story as a story bothered the Middle Ages very little. The important thing for them was that it was allegory, from which they could draw valuable moral lessons. This form of literature charmed them like a wizard's spell, and its influence was never more potent than in the thirteenth and fourteenth centuries. Even when in prose, it had something of the emotional stimulus of poetry. As Henry Osborn Taylor remarks, 'allegory became the chief field for the medieval imagination.'[2] Modern times have ceased completely to feel its fascination. As a living force in literature it is dead today, surviving only when the story has become the main interest, as in *Gulliver's Travels*, or when it commands attention for the perfection of its artistry, as in the *Divine Comedy*, or as a social document, in *Piers Plowman*.

What is the chief message of the *Melibeus*? At first sight, the tale seems to be that of a man sorely tried under adversity and at length, by the exercise of virtue, restored to happiness, like Job. Indeed, there is reason to suppose that the Book of Job may have influenced the invention of the simple plot. The author quotes from it; the question why God allows man to suffer cruel affliction is touched upon, and the symposium of the friends of Melibeus reminds us of the discourses of Eliphaz the Temanite and Bildad the Shuhite and Zophar the Naamathite. The Book of Job had of course been a favourite allegory in the Middle Ages ever since Pope Gregory the Great wrote his famous commentary. But Melibeus is not, like Job, a good man tested by the Lord (and Satan);[3] he is a man who has sinned. The allegory is clumsy enough, but its significance is clear from the words of Dame Prudence, who is at once an actor in the tale, and its expositor. Melibeus is the 'honey-drinker' who has tasted so much of temporal riches and delights that he is drunken; he has forgotten Christ, against whom he has sinned, so that the three enemies of man, the world, the

---

[1] J. S. P. Tatlock, *Development and Chronology of Chaucer's Works*, Chaucer Society, 1907, pp. 189–100.

[2] *A Historian's Creed*, Cambridge, Mass., 1939, p. 126.

[3] I do not forget that the motivation of the underlying folk tale has been much obscured by the processes of growth in the Book of Job. See Morris Jastrow, Jr., *The Book of Job; its Origin, Growth and Interpretation*, Philadelphia and London, 1920.

flesh, and the devil, have wounded his soul (his daughter Sophie) in five places, that is, through the five senses (Robinson, 213–214). So Dame Prudence says 'I conseille yow . . . aboven alle thynges, that ye make pees bitwene God and yow; and beth reconsiled unto hym and to his grace' (221). The allegory creaks a good deal at the end, when the goodwife sends for the three enemies and converts them to such sweet reasonableness that they are willing to make humble amends, and submit themselves to Melibeus. That is not the way the world, the flesh, and the devil usually treat a sinner, no matter how much prudence and wisdom he may display. However, the medieval man was not censorious; he took allegory as he found, it, and thanked God for what it taught him.

Much more striking than the significance of the *Melibeus* as an allegory of sin and God's forgiveness is its constant insistence that peace is better than war, and composition or legal punishment better than private vengeance. This, I believe, interested Albertanus chiefly, which was perhaps the reason why his allegory stumbled at the end. At first, Melibeus is all for violent measures: 'it seemed that in herte he baar a crueel ire, redy to doon vengeaunce upon his foes, and sodeynly desired that the werre shólde bigynne' (Robinson, 202). Then follows the best scene in the story, vividly set forth, and not overloaded with quotations until Dame Prudence begins to speak. Were it in verse, I venture to think that it would have been admired: as it is, real conviction and eloquence occasionally break through the crabbed prose. Melibeus has called together his friends, and asked their counsel. The physicians advise vengeance, and so do envious neighbours and feigned friends and flatterers. But 'an advocat that was wys' reminds them that to begin war and execute vengeance is not lightly to be undertaken. But most of those present, especially the young folk, cried out 'War! War!'

Up roos tho oon of thise wise, and with his hand made contenaunce that men sholde holden hem stille and yeven hym audience. 'Lordynges,' quod he, 'ther is ful many a man that crieth "Werre! werre!" that woot ful litel what werre amounteth. Werre at his bigynnyng hath so greet and entryng and so large, that every wight may entre whan hym liketh, and lightly fynde werre; but certes, what ende that shal therof bifalle, it is ʉat light to knowe. For soothly, whan that werre is ones bigonne, ther is ful many a child unborn of his mooder that shal sterve yong by cause of thilke werre, or elles lyve in sorwe and dye in wrecchednesse. And therfore, er that any werre bigynne, men moste have greet conseil and greet deliberacion.' (Robinson, 203)

It is plain that Melibeus, even after a long discourse from Dame Prudence, still stands for the principle of an eye for an eye and a tooth for a tooth.

'Certes,' quod Melibeus, 'I understonde it in this wise: that right as they han doon me a contrarie, right so sholde I doon hem another. For right as they han venged hem on me and doon me wrong, right so shal I venge me upon hem and doon hem wrong; and thanne have I cured oon contrarie by another.' (Robinson, 210)

But after much more eloquence from his spouse he is converted to a better way of thinking, so that at the end he is reconciled to his enemies and they to him, and he gives up all thought of vengeance. The importance of the general point was clearly seen by Sundby, in his excellent edition of the Latin text. He noted that Albertanus 'safely leads his readers to the goal he had proposed: condemnation of feuds and wilful wars, and submission to law. *This is the principal tendency of this book,* and very remarkable for the time when it was written.'[4] It is a pity that Sundby did not develop this further, and that its significance has not been seen by those who have endeavoured to explain the English *Melibeus*. In order to understand it fully we must consider the contemporary administration of justice, and the career of Albertanus.

Precisely the conflict which we trace in the *Melibeus* between private revenge and organized justice marks the development of law in the later Middle Ages. The earlier centuries had striven chiefly for the regulation of private vengeance, the systematization of penalties, and the termination of long-standing feuds. As time went on, and the power of the state increased, and the practical features of Roman law were better understood, the old Germanic concept of vengeance as the recognized method of inflicting punishment and gaining redress was gradually abandoned. The influence of the Church was particularly important; specifically through the 'Peace of God', which exempted certain parts of the community from warfare, and the 'Truce of God', which restricted times and seasons when war might be waged. In the thirteenth century, especially in the reign of Louis ix in France, these humanizing and liberalizing tendencies were marked in lay authority in the so-called *asseurement,* or suspension of hostilities by mutual consent of the contending parties, and in the *quarantaine du roi,* which set up a truce of forty days, and protected relatives not directly concerned in the original criminal action. Religion, ethics, and law are mingled in the arguments of Dame Prudence, as they were in medieval attempts to organize justice at this time. Reform of judicial procedure was especially affected by Christian teaching in the administration of a man of the deep and sincere piety of St Louis. He was far more powerful than many of his predecessors—he was really King of France, not merely an important noble among other contentious nobles. His influence and example spread far beyond the

---

[4] Sundby, p. xvii. Italics mine. I did not notice Sundby's remarks until after the first draft of this article was written. How they have escaped the attention of readers of the English text for so long I do not see. Possibly they have received attention in criticism which I have overlooked.

boundaries of his own kingdom. In 1258 he endeavoured to interdict private warfare altogether in France, but without complete success. The old custom of private vengeance was not to be abolished so quickly. Not until well into the fourteenth century was it effectively replaced by punishment at the hands of duly constituted authorities. Justice was often administered in a strange way, alternating between cruel severity and complete forgiveness—as we may observe in the closing pages of the *Melibeus*.[5] . . .

Viewed against this background, the *Melibeus* takes on, I think, a new significance. To men wearied of continual strife, in countries exhausted by internal struggle and foreign invasion, this parable, written by no monkish idealist but by an active citizen, judge, and military leader, expressed the hope of something better and finer in the administration of justice and the settlement of wars. We may recoil at its prolixity, we may yawn at its trite aphorisms, we may smile at its crude allegory, but we cannot deny that it shows a wisdom and a vision of which the thirteenth century stood sadly in need. It was no less timely in the age of Chaucer. The exhaustion and depression in England in the reign of Richard II are too familiar to need emphasis. How deeply the evils of war and the perversion of justice impressed Gower and Langland we know; can they have been absent from Chaucer's mind when he translated the *Melibeus?* May they not, indeed, have been one of the chief reasons why he made the translation?

From *Essays and Studies in Honour of Carleton Brown*, New York University Press and Oxford, 1940, pp. 101–109.

---

[5] For the legal situation in medieval France, and its reflection in imaginative literature, see F. Carl Riedel, *Crime and Punishment in the Old French Romances*, New York, 1938, esp. 11–43.

Select Bibliography

The Complete Works of Geoffrey Chaucer: edited by F. N. Robinson, Houghton Mifflin and Oxford University Press, 1933, second edition 1957. (The standard edition.)
The Oxford Chaucer: edited by W. W. Skeat, 6 volumes, Oxford, 1894–97.
The Complete Works of Geoffrey Chaucer: edited by W. W. Skeat, (Oxford Standard Authors), 1912.

There are other complete editions, and innumerable editions of separate texts; the most notable is *The Text of the Canterbury Tales,* edited by J. M. Manly and Edith Rickert, Chicago, 1940.

WORKS OF REFERENCE

W. F. Bryan and Germaine Dempster, *Sources and Analogues of Chaucer's* 'Canterbury Tales', Chicago, 1941.
Martin M. Crow and Clair C. Olsen (editors), *Chaucer Life-Records,* Clarendon Press, 1966.
D. D. Griffith, *A Bibliography of Chaucer 1908–53* (supplement *1954–63* by Wm. R. Crawford), Washington, 1953 and 1963.
Beryl Rowland (editor), *Companion to Chaucer Studies,* Oxford, 1968.
R. S. Loomis, *A Mirror of Chaucer's World,* Princeton, 1965. (Richly pictorial and descriptive account of what Chaucer saw around him.)
Edith Rickert, Clair C. Olsen, Martin M. Crow, *Chaucer's World,* Columbia and Oxford, 1948. (Documents relating to all aspects of life in Chaucer's time.)
Caroline F. E. Spurgeon, *Five Hundred Years of Chaucer Criticism and Allusion,* Cambridge, 1925.

CRITICISM (with emphasis on work published since about 1940)

Ralph Baldwin, 'The Unity of the Canterbury Tales', *Anglistica,* vol. 5, 1955.
Paull F. Baum, *Chaucer's Verse,* Duke University Press, 1961.

Dorothy Bethurum, 'Chaucer's Point of View as Narrator in the Love Poems', *Proceedings of the Modern Language Association,* vol. LXXIV, 1959.

Derek Brewer, *Chaucer in his Time,* Nelson, 1963.

Wolfgang H. Clemen, *Chaucer's Early Poetry,* Methuen, 1963.

Nevill Coghill, *The Poet Chaucer,* Clarendon Press, Oxford, Home University Library), 1949.

S. H. Cox, 'Chaucer's Cheerful Cynicism', *Modern Language Notes,* vol. XXXVI, 1921. (An unusual and interesting attack on Chaucer's attitude to life.)

D. S. Fansler, *Chaucer and the 'Roman de la Rose',* Columbia, 1914.

Robert D. French, *A Chaucer Handbook,* 1st edition, New York, 1927; 2nd edition, Bell and Son, 1947.

B. F. Huppé and D. W. Robertson, *Fruyt and Chaf: Studies in Chaucer's Allegories,* Princeton, 1963.

John Lawlor, *Chaucer,* Hutchinson, 1968.

John Livingston Lowes, *Geoffrey Chaucer,* Oxford, 1934; re-issued Clarendon Press, 1944.

R. M. Lumiansky, *Of Sondry Folk: the dramatic principle in the 'Canterbury Tales',* University of Texas, 1955.

Kemp Malone, *Chapters on Chaucer,* Johns Hopkins, 1951.

J. M. Manly, *Chaucer and the Rhetoricians,* Warton Lecture on English Poetry no. 17, 1926 (Proceedings of the British Academy).

Charles Muscatine, *Chaucer and the French Tradition,* Berkeley, 1957.

H. R. Patch, *On Re-reading Chaucer,* Harvard, 1939.

R. O. Payne, *Chaucer and the Shape of Creation,* Harvard and Oxford, 1967.

D. W. Robertson, *A Preface to Chaucer,* Princeton and Oxford, 1963.

R. K. Root, *The Poetry of Chaucer,* Houghton Mifflin, 1906, revised edition, 1922. (Still one of the best of all general introductions to Chaucer.)

Richard J. Schoeck and Jerome Taylor (editors), *Chaucer Criticism,* 2 volumes, Indiana, 1960–61.

John Spiers, *Chaucer the Maker,* Faber and Faber, 1951.

John S. P. Tatlock, *The Mind and Art of Chaucer,* Syracuse, New York, 1st edition 1950, 2nd edition 1966.

Edward Wagenknecht (editor), *Chaucer: Modern Essays in Criticism,* Oxford, 1959.